Activities for Teaching
Social Skills, Self Management & Respectful Living

Susanna Palomares

Dianne Schilling

Copyright © 2011 by Innerchoice Publishing • All rights reserved

ISBN - 10: 1-56499-080-8

ISBN - 13: 978-1-56499-080-8

INNERCHOICE Publishing
15079 Oak Chase Court
Wellington, FL 33414

www.InnerchoicePublishing.com

Activity sheets may be reproduced in quantities sufficient for distribution to students in education and counseling programs utilizing *Activities for Teaching Social Skills, Self Management, and Respectful Living*. All other reproduction, in any manner or for any purpose whatsoever, is explicitly prohibited without written permission. Request for such permission should be directed to INNERCHOICE PUBLISHING.

Contents

INTRODUCTION 5

We're All in the Same Boat 11
Hands of Respect 14
Respect All Around 16
Respect for the Animals 18
How I Show Respect for Myself 20
What's Wrong with Cheating? 22
Trusting Me, Trusting You 25
Honesty Is the Best Policy 28
Expressing Gratitude 31
It's the Thought That Counts 35
Heart Power 39
Recognizing the Needs of Others 42
Responsible and Dependable 47
Who Is Responsible? 50
Caring in the News 55
Taking Control of Anger 57
When It's Right to Say No 60
We're All Different - and the Same 64
Five Things We All Like 66
No Room for Stereotypes 67
Fighting Prejudice, Stereotypes and Discrimination 71
Nonviolent Communication 73
Win-Win Role Play 79
How to Make a New Friend 82
Speaking Out Against Bullying 85
No More Put Downs 88
Gossip Hurts 90
Making the Right Decision 92
What Is the Right Thing to Do? 95

Introduction

Children and young people who are respectful of self and others, manage their own feelings and behaviors well, and who relate effectively to others are at an advantage in all life endeavors: school, sports, community, family life, and work. They are also more likely to lead happy, productive lives. In order to help create an environment that enhances social competence and helps children develop respect for self and others a wide range of activities with social and emotional themes are provided in this activity guide.

Research reported in the journal "Child Development" indicates that developing these skills not only helps kids to get along better in life, but that they also improve their grades and standardized test scores by as much as 11 percentile points compared to kids without instruction in social and emotional learning.

The wide range of social-emotional learning activities in this book address a number of critical life skills including:

- Empathy
- Kindness
- Respect
- Trust
- Honesty
- Gratitude
- Fairness
- Compassion
- Problem solving
- Responsibility
- Decision making
- Self-control
- Tolerance
- Inclusion

Engaging Empathy

First and foremost, the activities are designed to engage the innate capacity of students to empathize with the feelings of others. Empathy is among the first emotions to develop. Even toddlers try to comfort one another. Empathic children can sense, identify with, and understand what other children are feeling. They can almost get inside the heads and hearts of their peers, connecting and relating to their needs.

When a student feels and expresses empathy for a friend whose feelings have been hurt by an unkind action, the student learns that actions have consequences, and that how people behave toward one another can cause a range of emotions, including the friend's (and the student's own) pain.

Since empathy is a key emotion supporting the development of social and emotional skills, its development is a major focus of the activities in this book. Throughout the activities, students are asked to imagine themselves in the place of others, and to describe how others feel due to various events or circumstances.

Numerous dyad and small group activities promote empathic listening. Storytelling and role-playing are also employed, along with what-if scenarios that help students express their sense of empathy and ideas for getting along with others.

Empathy plays an important role in ethical decision-making. When an activity calls for the evaluation of alternatives, in a variety of ways students are asked, "How would this alternative affect each person who is involved?" To answer that question effectively, students must exercise empathy.

Taking Advantage of Teachable Moments

When a student is being respectful, fulfilling a responsibility in a timely manner, or treating another student kindly, draw attention to the behavior, either by voicing your appreciation privately, or in the presence of others. Emphasize the consequences of the behavior. For example, suppose a student returns a borrowed key promptly. What are the consequences? You save time by not having to track it down. Your trust in the student grows. You are more likely to loan other items to the student. Whatever is true for you, share that information with the student.

Do the same with behaviors that affect others negatively. For example, if a student shares a confidence outside the group, discuss how that undermines trust and how other students might hesitate to share their thoughts in the future.

Teachable moments don't necessarily involve students directly. They can be incidents that have occurred elsewhere on campus or in the community. News reports yield an endless supply of teachable moments provided you discuss them with the students right away, while the news is still current. Encourage students to bring in reports that disturb or puzzle them.

Develop an ear for conflict and relationship dilemmas, which present themselves daily in the narratives of students, colleagues, friends and family. Jot down the details, change the names, and ask your students to solve them. This provides fertile ground for developing moral judgment and problem-solving skills.

The ultimate goal of the activities in this book is for children to develop skills for living well in all aspects of their lives. Relate teachable moments to previous activities, or slip them into the activity of the day.

Leading by Example

Kids learn more about social competence, self management, and respectful living from the day-to-day operations of the school and classroom than they do from any formal lesson. They learn from counselors and teachers who greet them by name as they enter the classroom, who include them in rule making, foster democratic classrooms, and demonstrate warmth and caring. They learn from principals who are visible and active, who talk to them respectfully, who demonstrate fairness and attempt to correct misguided or unworkable policies.

Decide what skills and values are important to you, and then model what you want the students to do. To the degree that you empathize with the feelings and needs of students, they will work to empathize with the feelings and needs of others. To the degree that you seek their point of view, they will listen to the views of others. To the degree that you are candid and open with them, they will have the courage to be honest with one another.

When leading the activities, don't hesitate to share your own experiences. Talk about the feelings you have had in various situations, the situations in life you've struggled with, the choices you've made and the consequences of those choices, both good and bad.

Cultivating Social Interaction

It seems obvious that nothing promotes social development better than social experience, and since peer relations is the primary preoccupation of children as they approach adolescence, go with that current. Be there to encourage thinking, discussion and debate about relationship issues as they arise. Intervene in social disputes and help students solve their own problems.

Hold group meetings to make decisions and settle conflicts. When a disagreement is between a small number of students, obtain the permission of the disputants before opening a problem to the entire group. Model respect. Create a supportive forum, not a tribunal.

Ask questions to help students reach conclusions and make decisions. Formulate open-ended questions that require thoughtful responses. Ask, "What would happen if you tried…?" "Why is solution A fairer than solution B?" "When you put yourself in John's place, what feelings or ideas do you have?" All of the activities in this book include discussion questions to stimulate thinking and idea sharing. Be sure to use them.

Encourage the students to ask questions too. Invite them to challenge one another's thinking, and yours. Create a trusting atmosphere where students feel comfortable posing their own dilemmas and asking "What should I do?"

Use whole class, small-group and individual activities in relatively equal numbers. Children, like adults, benefit from a blend of small group intimacy, large group stimulation, and solitary contemplation. Their brains operate differently in each genre. In this book, you will find almost every conceivable grouping—individual exercises, dyads, triads, and larger combinations.

Group students in ways that allow them to appreciate one another's strengths. Research has shown that children whose experiences are limited, who are not exposed to people of different races and cultures for instance, may not develop empathy for those people. Broadening a student's exposure is called "bridging," and creates a more accepting and tolerant child.

Using the Activities

Each activity in this guidebook is designed to explore and exercise one or more social and emotional skill. The activities are grouped according to those skills, but are not otherwise sequential. Each activity can stand alone.

The level of difficulty varies. If you like an activity, but think that the presentation is too sophisticated for your students, find ways to modify it. Simplify the vocabulary, revise the explanations, give examples that the students will find familiar.

There are several ways to use the activities. One way is to implement them in more or less the order presented over a period of weeks or months. For example, you might decide to do one activity each week. Another way is to let particular issues determine the order. For example, if you want your students to explore Responsibility, choose one or more activities that will promote that objective.

Feel free to modify the activities to suit the maturity, reading ability, culture and interests of your students. Apply your own expertise as well. Enhancements based on your knowledge and experience are welcomed and encouraged.

Many of the activities call for the use of supporting skills, including listening skills, decision making, problem solving, conflict resolution, and perspective taking. To a limited extent, these skills are explained as their use is employed. However, you may determine that your students need a more thorough introduction. Take the time to teach and practice skills that your students are unfamiliar with. For example, talk about the characteristics of good listening, the steps in a sound decision-making process, and how to conduct necessary research before evaluating alternatives.

Finally, every activity includes a list of discussion questions. These questions are a vital component of the activity. They give the students an opportunity to summarize and reflect on what they have learned, to compare their choices with other alternatives, and to explore various consequences.

During discussion, the students translate experiential learning into cognitive understanding and commit concepts to long term memory. If you omit the discussion following an activity, you run the risk of nullifying the experience. If the set of questions provided proves less than relevant to what your students learned by doing the activity, create your own open-ended, thought-provoking discussion questions that hit the mark.

We're All in the Same Boat

If civilization is to survive, we must cultivate the science of human relationships—the ability of all peoples, of all kinds, to live together in the same world, at peace.
—FRANKLIN D. ROOSEVELT

Objectives

The students will:
1. Recognize that regardless of our backgrounds, we live interdependent lives.
2. Understand the role of kindness in living interdependently.
3. Identify kind deeds that they have done for others.
4. Recognize the kind deeds of their classmates.

Materials

Large sheet of construction or contact paper for bulletin board "boat;" one copy of the experience sheet, "A Kind Act," for each student; pens, crayons, or markers

Procedure

On a large sheet of construction or contact paper, draw a simple boat. Cut out the boat and attach it to a bulletin board. Write the following quote on the side of the boat:

"We may have all come on different ships, but we're in the same boat now."
—Martin Luther King, Jr.

Ask for several interpretations of this quote. Give students a brief overview of King's leadership of the civil rights movement of the 1960s. Emphasize his lifelong desire to see change occur peacefully and to have all people be accepted as worthwhile individuals.

Talk about the role of kindness in King's vision of acceptance, equality and interdependence. Explain that being kind means reaching out to others with warmth, consideration and generosity. In some instances it might mean lending a helping hand. In others it might mean offering praise or a compliment.

Ask the students to help you come up with some examples of kind deeds. For example:

- Returning a shopping cart for someone
- Picking up trash on the school grounds
- Writing a letter of appreciation to a person who made a difference in your life
- Watering the neighbors' garden while they are on vacation
- Sharing your snack with someone
- Showing a classmate how to solve a math problem
- Holding the door for someone pushing a wheelchair or stroller
- Donating some of your allowance or earnings to charity
- Offering to wash your elderly neighbor's car

Explain that each time the students do something like this, even though it is small, they are helping to make the world a kinder place.

Have the students complete their experience sheets by filling in the silhouette with facial features and other details, and by writing a kind deed they have done for someone in the heart area. Have them cut out their completed illustrations.

One by one, or a few at a time, have the children fill the large boat on the bulletin board with their likenesses.

Take a few minutes each day to look at several of the figures, enjoy the resemblance they have to the student they represent, and discuss the larger significance of the deed described.

Ask the discussion questions at any appropriate time during the activity.

Discussion Questions

1. What does it mean to be kind?
2. Why is it important to be kind?
3. How do you feel when someone is kind to you?
4. How do you feel when you are kind to someone?
5. How do you feel when someone is unkind to you?
6. What are some examples of unkind behavior?
7. What causes people to be kind or unkind?
8. What should you do when you see someone being unkind to a person or animal?
9. If we value kindness, is it our responsibility to encourage other people to be kind? How should we do that?

A Kind Act

Draw and color this silhouette to look like you.
In the heart area, write one kind act that you have done for someone.

Hands of Respect

The 3 Rs:
Respect for self,
Respect for others,
Responsibility for all your actions

Objectives

The students will:
1. Identify respectful actions.
2. Describe an incident in which they demonstrated respect.
3. Creatively symbolize expressions of respect.

Materials

Art paper; colored markers or crayons; glue; decorative materials such as stickers, sequins, buttons, etc. (optional)

Procedure

Begin by asking the students to think of things that people do to show respect for one another. Focus on small courtesies like greeting a person, saying please and thank you, holding a door, letting someone go first, and shaking hands. Tell the children:

I've heard that some coaches insist that their players shake hands with the members of the opposing team after every game, regardless of whether they win or lose.

- *Why would a coach do that?*
- *What message does the coach want to send the other team?*
- *What do the players learn by doing this?*

After the children have had a few minutes to talk about this display of respect, announce that they are going to participate in an activity about respect, but in this activity instead of shaking hands, they'll draw hands.

Have the students form dyads. Distribute the art materials.

Instruct the children to take turns tracing each other's hand on a sheet of art paper. Point out that the drawing they end up with will not be of their own hand, but of their partner's hand. When they have finished tracing, explain the next step (in your own words).

Interview your partner to find out how your partner shows respect for other people. See if your partner can remember a specific time when he or she said or did something that demonstrated respect for a particular person. Take notes on your scratch paper. Then let your partner interview you. When both of you have finished, use what you've learned to illustrate the tracing of your partner's hand to show the respectful things your partner does. Use letters, symbols, pictures, and other decorations. Your illustration can symbolize lots of respectful actions, or it can tell the story of one particular incident. Decide who will be the first interviewer and get started.

List the following questions on the board to assist the students during their interviews:

Interview Questions

- *How do you show respect for other people?*
- *Can you remember a specific time when you did something for another person that showed respect? What happened?*

Have the entire group sit in a circle. Go around the circle and have the students introduce their partner by showing their hand drawing and describing their partner's respectful actions.

Lead a culminating group discussion. Later, display the hand drawings on a bulletin board, or create a class book of all the hand drawings.

Discussion Questions

1. *A picture of two hands shaking is often used as a symbol of mutual respect and understanding. Why do you think that is?*
2. *What are some other ways of showing respect that we included in our drawings?*
3. *If you offered to shake someone's hand and that person refused, what would you think?*
4. *Why is it important to show respect for others?*
5. *What would life be like if no one showed respect for anyone else?*

Respect All Around

Every part of this earth is sacred to my people; Every shining pine needle, every sandy shore, every mist in the dark woods, every clearing and humming insect is holy in the memory and experience of my people.
—CHIEF SEATTLE, 1885
...IN A LETTER TO THE PRESIDENT OF THE UNITED STATES

Objectives

The students will:
1. Define six types of respect (self-respect, respect for others, respect for property, respect for authority, respect for the environment and respect for animals).
2. Share examples showing why each type of respect is important.

Materials

Colored construction paper; newsprint or other plain paper for each student

Procedure

Have the students brainstorm different meanings of respect. Write the meanings on the board. Include:

- Self-respect
- Respect for others
- Respect for property
- Respect for authority
- Respect for the environment
- Respect for animals

Discuss each kind of respect with the students.

Divide the students into six groups and assign each group one type of respect. Have each group write a short statement defining their category of respect and list examples of times when they have demonstrated that type of respect. Finally, have them write why their type of respect is important.

Assemble the individual pages into a book. Choose volunteers to design and produce a cover for the book.

Share the book with a primary class to help them understand respect.

Discussion Questions

1. How does it feel when someone shows you respect?
2. How does it feel when you act respectfully toward an adult?
3. Are people in our school respectful of each other? Why or why not?
4. What is an example of property we should respect?
5. Why is it sometimes difficult to respect people in authority?
6. Is there ever a time when a student should not respect an older person?... When?
7. When is it hard to respect yourself?
8. Why is respecting yourself important?
9. What are the benefits of respecting the environment?
10. How can you show respect for the environment?
11. Why do animals deserve respect?
12. How do animals show their understanding when you respect them?

Variation

If computers and publishing software are available, encourage the children to work in teams using these tools to produce the pages and cover of the book.

Respect for the Animals

Our task must be to free ourselves...
by widening our own circle of compassion
to embrace all living creatures and
the whole of nature and its beauty.
ALBERT EINSTEIN

Objectives

The students will:
1. Research the plight of an endangered animal.
2. Describe humanity's responsibility to protect animals from extinction.
3. Demonstrate personal responsibility by helping an endangered animal.

Materials

Reference books and resources (from internet, libraries, etc) containing information about animals currently on the endangered list; pencils, writing paper, poster paper, colored markers, paper mache or clay, tempera paint, and paint brushes

Procedure

Begin this activity with a discussion of humanity's responsibility to animals. Talk about how humans have over-hunted animals and destroyed their habitats so that some are endangered. Get a list of the animals currently considered endangered form the local zoo or from web sites on the internet like Kids Planet (www.kidsplanet.org) or the World Wildlife Fund (www.worldwildlife.org). Copy the list on the board, and discuss why some of the animals have been hunted to the extent that they are almost extinct. Explain, for example: *The Indian White Rhinoceros is hunted for its horn, which is said to have magical powers. In fact, the horn is composed of the same material that makes up our hair and fingernails. It is an endangered animal. Elephants are hunted for their ivory tusks and are becoming endangered. Other animals, like the leopard, are hunted for their beautiful fur, and are dwindling in numbers. The Giant Panda is endangered because humans are destroying its habitat and food supply.*

Ask that every student choose one animal to be the subject of a personal "research and help" project.

Have the students read books and magazines and conduct internet research to gain more information on their endangered animal. Suggest that they take careful notes, which will help them explain why their animal is endangered, and will suggest ways they can aid the animal.

After the research period, have the students tell the class some of what they learned.

Ask the students to think of something they can do to help the animal. Suggest, for example: *Write a letter urging the president or government head of the country where the animal lives to do all he or she can to save the animal. Write letters to the government heads of countries where the endangered animal is hunted, and request that the hunting be stopped. Make a poster showing the endangered animal, and caption it with information about the causes of the animals's peril. Ask a local merchant to put the poster in his or her store window. Make an animal sculpture out of clay or paper mache, paint it, and then place the sculpture in a shoe-box diorama showing its healthy, safe environment. Label the display and place it in the school office or library for all to see.*

Allow the students to report on their projects and describe how they plan to help save their endangered animals. Discuss other actions they might take in the future.

Discussion Questions

1. *How do you feel about having assumed some responsibility for helping an endangered animal?*
2. *How can people solve the problem of animal endangerment and extinction?*
3. *What was the most important thing you learned from this activity?*

How I Show Respect for Myself

Respect your efforts, respect yourself. Self respect leads to self discipline. When you have both firmly under your belt, that's real power.
CLINT EASTWOOD

Objectives:

The students will
1. Describe ways in which they show respect for themselves.
2. Recognize various other ways to show respect for one's self.

Materials:

One copy of the experience sheet, "How I Show Respect for Myself," for each student

Procedure:

Duplicate the experience sheet and give each student a copy. Briefly review the directions. Make sure that the students understand the concept that self respect, and the lack of it, are readily demonstrated in behavior. That liking and respecting oneself are not just feelings, they are actions.

In each category, have the students write at least one thing they do to demonstrate respect for themselves. When they are finished, allow the students to share what they have written with a partner or in small groups.

Lead a discussion. Ask the students these and other open-ended questions to stimulate further thinking:

Discussion Questions:

1. *What is respect?*
2. *How is respecting yourself similar to respecting your parents, your flag, or your principal? How is it different?*
3. *Which part of the experience sheet was hardest to complete? Why?*
4. *Why is it important to show respect for yourself as well as for others?*
5. *What have you learned from this activity?*

Conclude the activity. Suggest that the students take their experience sheets home and share them with a parent or other caregiver.

How I Show Respect for Myself

Respecting yourself means that you think positively about yourself and treat yourself well. In each category below, write one or more activities that you do regularly to demonstrate that you respect yourself.

I respect my body:

Nutrition: _____
_____

Exercise: _____
_____

Hygiene: _____
_____

Sleep: _____
_____

Grooming: _____
_____

I respect my mind:

Study habits:
_____
_____

New things I am learning:
_____
_____

What I am curious about:
_____
_____

I respect my feelings:

How I express my feelings: _____

How I reduce stress: _____

How I make myself feel happy: _____

I respect my behavior:

Good habits I have: _____

How I manage my time: _____

Things I say: _____

What's Wrong with Cheating?

Honesty is contagious, just like dishonesty is contagious.
We need more honesty in the world.
—ANNE WILSON SCHAEF

Objectives

The students will:
1. Describe various forms of cheating.
2. Explain the negative consequences of cheating
3. Recognize that cheating hurts everyone, including the cheater.

Materials

Large pieces of butcher paper; drawing paper, art supplies and writing implements

Procedure

Begin by asking the children: *Do you know what cheating is?*

Discuss the meaning of cheating, inviting the students to share their perceptions. Add to their ideas by explaining that cheating is getting something in a dishonest way. Ask the students to think of some examples of cheating in school. List their suggestions on the board, adding ideas of your own. The list should include:

— copying answers from someone else's paper instead of doing your own work.
— erasing someone's name from a paper and putting your own name on it.
— taking the teacher's answer book and getting answers to an assignment.
— getting someone else to do your work for you.
— getting something off the Internet and calling it your own work.
— breaking rules in a game in order to win points.

Have the students form groups of three or four. Explain that their task is to brainstorm as many reasons as they can think of why cheating is wrong.

Have them focus on the possible effects, or consequences, of cheating in school.

Give each group a sheet of butcher paper and a colored marker. Ask them to select a scribe to record their ideas in large lettering on the butcher paper. Allow 5 to 10 minutes to complete the task. When time is up, ask one member from each group to report to the whole class. Post the lists around the room.

If the following "reasons why cheating is wrong" are not included on the student lists, discuss them with the students while recording them on a separate list of your own. Post this list also.

- You lose the teacher's trust that you will do your own work.
- If you cheat in school, you may find it easier to cheat outside of school.
- Cheating is a lie because it causes people to think you know more than you do.
- Cheating may lead to other forms of lying.
- Cheating is not fair to students who are honest.
- If you get into the habit of cheating when you are young, you will find it easier to cheat when you are older.
- Cheating is taking something that you haven't earned, and may lead to other forms of stealing.
- You cheat yourself by not learning as much.

Announce that the students are going to have an opportunity to express one of their ideas about cheating in poster form. Distribute the art materials. Suggest that the students choose one "reason why cheating is wrong" from the posted lists and try to express that idea in as few words as possible, combining the words with a picture or symbol to complete the poster. For example, the words might read:

Choose to Cheat? Lose Self-Respect!
Cheating Is Lying
Cheating—Unfair to Others!
Cheat in School? Cheat Out of School!
Young Cheaters Become Old Cheaters

When the posters are finished, invite the students to share them with the class. Then display the posters on a bulletin board in the school auditorium or library under the heading, "Cheating Is Wrong Because..."

Conclude the activity with a discussion.

Discussion Questions

1. *How would you feel if someone cheated on a test and got a better score than you?*
2. *How would you feel if someone took your work and put his or her name on it?*
3. *How does cheating hurt the community? ...the country? ....the world?*
4. *How does cheating hurt the cheater?*
5. *Why do you think people cheat?*
6. *If you cheated on a test and got a score you know you didn't deserve, how would you feel?*

Variations

If you are working with younger students, allow the children to brainstorm their ideas while you record them on the board. Write a list of five or six short phrases for the children to choose from when making their posters.

Trusting Me, Trusting You

What lies behind us and what lies before us are tiny matters compared to what lies within us.
—OLIVER WENDELL HOMES

Objectives

The students will:
1. Identify specific ways in which people trust one another.
2. Name specific ways in which they trust individual classmates.
3. Explain why it is important for people to trust one another.
4. Define trust and explain in simple terms how it develops.

Materials

The experience sheet, "Trust Me"

Procedure

Make four copies of the experience sheet. Write the first names of one-fourth of your students on each sheet (randomly mixed), one name on each of the blank lines after the words "I trust." Duplicate the prepared copies for distribution (one version per child).

Ask the students to help you brainstorm some of the many different ways people trust one another in the classroom and elsewhere. List their ideas on the board. To facilitate, ask such questions as, "What do you trust each other for?" "What do you trust me for? "What do you trust your parents for? "What do you trust your neighbors for?" "What do you trust law enforcement officers for?"

Write their ideas on the board. Include such items as:

I trust _____ to keep a secret.

...tell the truth.
...return anything he or she borrows.
...be fair in games
...protect me.
...do a good job.
...be on time.
...keep a promise.

Distribute the experience sheets. Explain that you have divided up the names of class members so that everyone's name is on a sheet, but no sheet has all of the names. Tell the children that you want them to think about the unique qualities, talents and abilities of each person listed on their sheet and write down one way in which they trust that person. Tell them to use the list on the board for ideas and help with spelling. Circulate and provide assistance, as needed.

When the children have finished, ask those whose names are on the first list to come to the front of the room. Stand behind one student at a time and ask: "What do you trust John for?" Call on individual students to read what they have written. Repeat this process with the groups and students whose names are on the remaining lists.

Draw a line across the length of the board. At one end, write the label "Zero Percent Trust." At the other end of the line, write, "100 Percent Trust." Mark 25 Percent, 50 Percent, and 75 Percent as well.

Explain that the line represents a "continuum," and that each person falls somewhere on this line. Some people might put you at the low end, some people might put you in the middle, and others might put you in the high end. They really trust you.

Have the students write their names on the continuum showing where they think most people would place them. If time remains, ask them to put their names where *they* perceive themselves. Discuss the differences in the perceptions of themselves versus others.

Discussion Questions

1. How do you feel knowing that you can trust so many people?
2. How do we learn to trust other people?
3. How do you let others know they can trust you?
4. How does knowing you can count on someone build trust?
5. What is trust?
6. Why is trust important in friendships?... in families?... in our group?

Trust Me!

I trust _____ to _____
_____.

I trust _____ to _____
_____.

I trust _____ to _____
_____.

I trust _____ to _____
_____.

I trust _____ to _____
_____.

I trust _____ to _____
_____.

I trust _____ to _____
_____.

I trust _____ to _____
_____.

I trust _____ to _____
_____.

I trust _____ to _____
_____.

My classmates can trust me to:

1. _____
_____

2. _____
_____

3. _____
_____

Honesty Is the Best Policy

If you tell the truth, you don't need to remember anything.
—UNKNOWN

Objectives

The students will:
1. Define honesty and dishonesty
2. Discuss a variety of ways in which people show honesty or dishonesty.
3. Demonstrate how one lie often leads to others.

Materials

An 8-inch wide pot or bucket that can comfortably hold 8 inches of water; 1 quarter and 5 pennies

Procedure

Write the headings "Honesty" and "Dishonesty" on the board or chart paper. Ask the children to help you define both terms. Write down their ideas. Under honesty, include:

- Telling the truth
- Keeping promises
- Not exaggerating
- Admitting mistakes
- Accepting responsibility

Under dishonesty, include:

- Telling lies
- Exaggerating
- Breaking promises
- Covering up mistakes
- Making excuses

Discuss the following examples.

— *If you break a vase, and then tell your parent, "Maybe the cat knocked it over," is that being honest or dishonest?*
— *If you promise to meet a friend, and don't show up because you get busy doing something else, is that being honest or dishonest?*

— *If you say you won 15 times playing video games, when you only won five times, is that being honest?*
— *If you haven't finished studying, but you tell your mom you have so she'll let you watch your favorite TV show, is that being honest?*
— *What if you study later, after the TV show. Does that make it all right?*

Now write the heading "Consequences," under (or next to) your cumulative definition of honesty. Ask the students if they know what a consequence is. If some are doubtful, explain that a consequence is something that happens as a result of something else. For example, a consequence of studying is getting a better grade. Ask the students to think of consequences of being honest. List things like:

— People trust you.
— People respect and like you.
— You build a good reputation.
— You feel good about yourself.

Ask the students to think of the consequences of being dishonest. List things like:

— People are afraid to ask you to do things.
— People hesitate to tell you things.
— You lose friends.
— You build a bad reputation.
— You feel guilty.
— You worry about being discovered.

Now add another consequence that the children may not think of. Write:

— You have to tell more lies to cover up the first one.

Explain that you are going to play a little game to illustrate what happens when one lie grows into several.

Fill the container with six to eight inches of water. Tell the following story. Place the coins in the water at the indicated times.

Story

Monica wants to hang out at the mall with her friends after school, but she knows her mom won't approve, so she says that she has to stay late for a drama club rehearsal (quarter). At dinner, her mom asks how the rehearsal went, and Monica says fine (penny). Then her father asks what the club is rehearsing, so Monica thinks fast and says they are practicing some skits the kids made up (penny). When her mother asks if everyone had to make up a skit, Monica says yes (penny). Monica's little brother asks what her skit was about, and she mumbles, "Oh, nothing you'd be interested in. We didn't rehearse mine anyway." (penny) But her family is interested so they press her for details. Feeling trapped, she pretends to feel sick and leaves the table (penny).

State:

Trying to cover up a lie is a lot like trying to cover up this quarter with pennies. One usually isn't enough, so you have to keep telling lies to make sure that the other person doesn't discover the truth.

Have the children form pairs and make up their own stories about covering up a lie. Explain that they can base their stories on true experiences that they or someone they know have had. Then have them tell their stories while dropping the coins into the container.

Caution: Don't let the game-like atmosphere leave children with the impression that lying is fun. While it's true that covering up lies calls for creativity and invention, these attributes can also be developed by solving problems responsibly and honestly.

Discussion Questions

1. Why do people tell lies?
2. Is lying ever acceptable? When?
3. Who is the biggest loser when you lie? Why?

Variations

Act out the stories in pairs, with one person playing the part of the liar, and the other playing the other roles.

Expressing Gratitude

Life is not so short but that there is always time enough for courtesy.
—RALPH WALDO EMERSON

Objectives

The students will:
1. Identify things they are grateful for.
2. Distinguish between gratitude for the product and gratitude for the effort and feelings that produced the product.
3. Describe specific ways they demonstrate gratitude.

Materials

Binding machine or stapler; colored construction paper in 11 X 17 sheets (one per child, plus extras); 7 duplicates of the experience sheet, "I Am Grateful for Many Things," for each child; marking pens in various colors

Procedure

Engage the children in a discussion about what it means to be grateful.

Ask:

— *What do you think of when you hear the words "grateful" or "thankful"?*
— *Why do we talk about thankfulness so much in November?*
— *Do we express our gratitude enough during the rest of the year? Why or why not?*

Ask the students to name some of the things they are grateful for and how they show their gratitude. List a few of their responses on the board. Younger students are apt to name possessions, like toys, books, clothes, sports equipment and pets. To encourage the students to broaden their perception of gratitude, tell them the following story:

Cliff decided to surprise his mother, Melanie, by fixing dinner. He worked for several hours to prepare her favorite stew. When Melanie got home from work, the table was set and everything was ready. Cliff and his older brother,

Rick, sat down with Melanie at the table. She ate heartily, praising Cliff's efforts and thanking him for the wonderful stew. After dinner, Rick found some time to talk with his mother alone. He said, "Mom, that stew was awful. The meat was tough and the vegetables were overcooked." She said, "I know." Rick was puzzled. "Well, if you didn't like it, why did you keep thanking Cliff for it?" Melanie put her arm around Rick's shoulders and said, "I wasn't grateful for the stew itself, I was grateful for the hours Cliff spent fixing the stew. Do you see the difference? I'm so grateful for the love that inspired his gift, I don't care what the stew tasted like."

Ask:

— *What was Cliff's mom grateful for?*
— *What are you grateful for that can't be found in a store, or purchased at any price?*
— *How do you show your gratitude for these gifts?*

Again, list ideas on the board. Encourage the students to think about family, friends, special moments, celebrations, the time others spend teaching and caring for them, little favors, and other intangibles.

Distribute the experience sheets and other materials. Have the students make journals by inserting one experience sheet for each day of the week (4 sheets for double-sided duplication, 7 for single-sided) into folded 11 X 17 sheets of construction paper and stapling or binding the edges.

Have the students illustrate the covers of their journals. On the inside, have them label each page with a day of the week.

Explain to the students that they are to list at least three things each day that they are grateful for. In the second column, they are to describe how they showed their appreciation. As an alternative to writing, tell the students that they may draw each scenario.

At the end of the week, or at the next session, have the students take turns sharing all or parts of their journal with the group.

Discussion Questions

1. Why is it important to show gratitude and appreciation for the things we have?
2. Is there someone you have never thanked who you would like to thank now? If so, when and how will you do that?
3. How do people seem to feel when you show them your gratitude?
4. How do you feel when you express gratitude for something?

Variations

If the students have access to computer publishing software, allow them to design and print out their own journals, or work with two or three students to design and produce journals for the entire group.

I Am Grateful for Many Things

Day of the Week _____

Today I am grateful for...	How I show my gratitude...

It's the Thought That Counts

The best portion of a good man's life,
His little, nameless, unremembered acts of kindness and of love.
—WILLIAM WORDSWORTH

Objectives

The students will:
1. Understand the difference between being grateful for a gift and being grateful for the sentiment and effort behind the gift.
2. Explore feelings associated with giving and receiving.

Materials

One copy of the experience sheet, "The Gift," for each student

Procedure

Write the following sentence on the board: It's the thought that counts.

Ask:

— *Have you ever heard this expression? What does it mean?*

Discuss various interpretations of the expression, writing ideas on the board. Explain that this expression is usually used to acknowledge the feelings that motivated someone to do a thoughtful deed. Often the deed itself doesn't work out quite right, but that doesn't matter because "it's the thought that counts." Give some examples:

A girl bakes a birthday cake for her dad. The cake turns out flat and tasteless, but the dad is thrilled because of his daughter's thoughtfulness.

A grandmother takes the bus across town to bring her ailing grandchild a bag of candy. The child is too sick to eat sweets, but realizes that her grandmother just wants to make her happy.

A toddler loans her teddy bear to an elderly neighbor who just lost her husband. The neighbor has no use for the bear, but is touched by the child's caring gesture.

Ask:

— *Have you ever received a gift you didn't particularly like?*
— *Has your little brother or sister ever tried to make something for you and ended up making a big mess instead?*

Point out that in situations like this it's wise to look beyond (or behind) the results and appreciate the thought that motivated the deed, regardless of the outcome. Gratitude isn't just the thank-you note that your mother forces you to write. Its the feeling you get when you put yourself in the other person's shoes and visualize the effort they made.

Distribute the experience sheet and give the students a few minutes to read the story. Or have several students take turns reading portions of the story aloud. Afterwards, discuss the story and the lessons it teaches.

Discussion Questions

1. Why was Susanna unhappy living in Italy?
2. What were some of the challenges she faced?
3. Why didn't Nonno Beppe realize that the ice cream would melt in his pockets? Can you imagine never having seen ice cream before?
4. Why did this incident change Susanna's feelings?
5. Why was Nonno Beppe able to laugh at himself? What effect did all the laughter have on Susanna?
6. How do you feel when you give someone a gift and they don't seem to appreciate it?
7. What should you do if your parent gives you a different toy than the one you asked for, or an item of clothing that you don't like?
8. What should you do if a friend comes to your birthday party with no gift at all?
9. How can you show gratitude for the act of giving, even if you don't care for the gift?
10. Since the gift Susanna got was something she couldn't touch or feel, why did she still feel it was a gift?

Extension

Have the children write and/or draw a picture telling about a time they got a special gift with a deeper meaning.

Variations

If the story is beyond the reading ability of the majority of your students, read it to them. You may still want to give them copies to take home and share with their families.

Allow several students to develop a short play based on "The Gift." Have them research the look of a small Italian village in the 1950s and paint a backdrop on butcher paper, obtain a few props, and create simple costumes.

The Gift

There I was, seven years old and back in Italy, the land of my birth. Uprooted from my life in America, I was bundled off to Europe in a rush by my mother so she could recover and regroup after a traumatic divorce from my father.

Being a war bride in America had been trying. She needed the support of her family and their simple way of life. She was sad and lonely in America. Now I was feeling the same way in Italy.

I was living with my grandparents in their 300-year-old farmhouse in a tiny village high in the mountains north of Florence. My mother, needing medical care and rest, was staying in the city.

I was used to an American way of life. Now, suddenly, I was in a place that had changed little since the 18th century, living with people I didn't know and struggling to understand a language I had never spoken. I was used to television, riding in cars, bright lights at the flip of a switch, and indoor plumbing, none of which existed in this village. Here, plows were pulled by oxen, water came in buckets drawn from a spring, and houses were lighted with kerosene lamps. My grandmother cooked in the open fireplace, our bread was baked in the ancient community stone oven. Clothes were washed in the river, and the toilet was a village outhouse.

I missed my father, my bedroom, and all the people and things I was familiar with. I was homesick, lonely and scared. I cried a lot those first few days.

My grandparents and everyone else tried their best to ease the transition, but there was no TV to distract me—no toys, games, or books. Children played with nature's ornaments—stones, pebbles, sticks and the like.

The people of the village were all subsistence farmers. Days were spent growing, harvesting, storing, preparing and eating food. The old farmhouses were furnished with only the barest necessities. Life was simple, uncomplicated, lived at the most basic level and, for me, miserable.

One chilly fall day my grandfather, Nonno Beppe, announced that he was going to walk down the mountain (indeed he had no other way to go) and into the town of Baragazza, which had modern conveniences like electricity, running water, and shops. I was made to understand that the purpose of his trip was to bring back a special gift for me.

Perhaps I was starting to adjust to my new life just a little, because this stirred my interest and I felt a tinge of excitement. Although I didn't understand why, things suddenly didn't look quite so bleak and lonely. My seven-year-old mind began to hum with anticipation. What could this special gift be?

It was a long trudge down the mountain on a trail that was little more than a goat path. Because of the great distance and time involved, such trips were infrequent, never taken on the spur of the moment, and always had multiple purposes. But on this day Nonno Beppe's trip was just for me.

Nonno Beppe knew exactly which shop to visit. He had carried fresh vegetables down the mountain. These he traded for not one, but two gifts, which he carefully placed in the inside pockets of his heavy wool coat, one on either side. Then he prepared for the long trek home.

Walking back up the mountain took more time than going down. Although the air was cold by now, Nonno Beppe was sweating and had to rest often, but he knew my gifts were safe in his inside pockets.

It was after dark when he finally reached home, and the whole extended family—aunts, uncles and cousins—had gathered around the fireplace in anticipation of his return. When he burst through the door, he was flushed with excitement. I jumped up and down as he opened his coat, reached into his pockets and pulled out...two small, gooey sticks.

For a brief moment we looked at each other in surprise. I thought, "What's special about these messy little sticks?" and he must have thought, "They were ice cream when I put them in my pockets."

My uncles, who were a bit more familiar with 20th century delicacies, burst out laughing. They immediately understood that the ice cream had melted in the warmth of Nonno Beppe's pockets. My grandfather had never sampled ice cream in his whole life. His only thought was for me. He was certain that ice cream would make his little granddaughter, used to American luxuries, feel at home.

As we started to grasp what had happened, everyone began laughing hysterically—including me.

I didn't get any ice cream, but somehow it didn't matter. I couldn't explain it then, but at that moment something wonderful happened. In all the hilarity, I was transformed. My inner turmoil was replaced by a feeling of peace. I understood that these people loved me more than I'd realized—really loved me and were there for me.

The real gift I got from Nonno Beppe that day was the knowledge that what we do for others is not as important as caring enough to try. The ice cream might have been eaten and forgotten, but because it melted in the loving warmth of my grandfather's coat, I've had Nonno Beppe's greater gift every day of my life.

© 2005 Susanna Palomares

Heart Power

Wherever you go, go with all your heart.
—CONFUCIUS

Objectives

The students will:
1. Define compassion as a deep concern for, and desire to help others.
2. Practice identifying compassionate acts.
3. Recognize their classmates for compassionate behaviors.

Materials

One copy of the experience sheet, "Heart Power," for each student, 3x5 cards, paste or glue, marking pens in various colors

Procedure

Write the word *compassion* on the board and ask the students what it means. Record their ideas. Have a student check the dictionary and read the definition to the group. The following definition is from the American Heritage Dictionary:

A deep awareness of the suffering of another coupled with a wish to relieve it.

Point out that compassion is two-pronged. It involves feelings (sensitivity, empathy, sympathy, concern, tenderness), plus a desire to *act on* those feelings — to do something to help the other person. Compassion is not a passive emotion. It compels us to act.

Ask the students to describe compassionate behaviors that they have observed in the last few days. To get the process started, describe a specific compassionate act that you witnessed, such as one child comforting another, people administering aid to the victim of an accident, or someone adopting an animal from a shelter. Then call on volunteers to describe other compassionate acts.

Draw a heart shape on the board. Explain that we usually think of the heart as the center of compassion, just as we characterize love and sympathy as coming from the heart. We say things like:

She is speaking from her heart.

He has a good heart.

Their reaction was heartfelt.

Give one experience sheet and six 3x5 cards to each student. Explain that the heart shapes on the sheet will act as symbols of compassion. Go over the directions on the experience sheet. Then give the students time to color and decorate the hearts before cutting them out and pasting them to the 3x5 cards.

Have the students keep their cards and use them to recognize classmates who demonstrate compassion. Tell them to write their classmate's name and a brief description of the compassionate act on the card.

After publicly presenting the card to the classmate being recognized, include the card in a bulletin board display entitled, "Heart Power."

Discussion Questions

1. *How do you feel when someone shows you compassion?*
2. *The opposite of compassion is indifference—a complete lack of caring. What would life be like if everyone were indifferent to the problems of others?*
3. *Can you act compassionately even if you don't have the power to help the other person? How?*

Variations

Have the children draw pictures of themselves and their classmates using heart power.

Heart Power

1. Decorate and color the hearts.
2. Cut out the hearts and paste each one to a separate 3x5 card.
3. Use the cards to recognize classmates when they do something compassionate.
4. Write the name of the compassionate student and a brief description of his or her deed on the card.
5. Present the card to the compassionate student in front of the group or class and describe the compassionate act to the group.

Recognizing the Needs of Others

*Could a greater miracle take place than for us to look through
each others' eyes for an instant?*
—HENRY DAVID THOREAU

Objectives

The students will:
1. Understand the importance of empathy and how empathy is achieved.
2. Empathize with people in a variety of situations.

Materials

One copy of the experience sheets, "Empathy Is..." and "Empathy Practice," for each student

Time

Parts of two sessions

Procedure

Give a copy of the experience sheet, "Empathy Is...," to each student. Tell the students that they have 1 minute to translate the Braille sentence at the top of the sheet. Call time and have the students stop working.

Ask:

— *Did anyone complete the translation? If so, what does the sentence say?*

Call on volunteers to read their translations, If no one was able to translate the sentence in the allotted time (which is likely), acknowledge the difficulty of the task and write the correct translation on the board. (Translation: *Empathy is imagining yourself in another person's shoes and feeling what they feel.*)

Have the students write the correct translation in the space provided on the bottom of the experience sheet.

Ask:

— *How did you feel when you could not easily understand what you were reading?*

Encourage sharing. The point being to get the children to get in touch with their feelings and then to transpose those feelings to how others might feel in situations where they are unsure.

Call on volunteers. Discuss the similarity between the situation they faced with the Braille and the experience of a child who must adjust to a new culture with an unfamiliar language, or a child with a disability learning to perform a difficult skill. Ask:

—Did this experience help you empathize with the child who can't speak English, or the child who is physically challenged by a disability?

Talk about what it means to empathize with another person. Differentiate empathy from sympathy. Empathy is not feeling sorry for someone. Empathy is identifying with the person, feeling what they feel. For most people, empathy is not a well-developed response. Sometimes it requires conscious thought. Explain that the children may have to ask themselves, "What is this person feeling right now?" and "How would I feel in her situation?"

Read the Empathy Situations below to the students. After each one, ask the listed questions and call on volunteers to name their projected feelings. Write these on the board. Use their answers to generate discussion. For example, if a child says he would feel protective and angry as the parent of the immigrant child (first situation), ask "Why?" or "What thoughts led you to that conclusion?" Encourage the students to put themselves in the shoes of the various people—to really "get inside" their heads and hearts.

Empathy Situations

1. Luce is a new student at your school. She dresses differently from the other girls. Her clothes fit poorly and are not stylish. When the kids make fun of her and call her names, Luce tells her parents. Her father visits the school to find out what is going on. How would you feel if you were 1) Luce, 2) Luce's father, 3) the school principal?

2. Marcie Brown and her children buy a house on a large lot next to a big apartment complex. They discover that the apartments' drainage ditch crosses the back of their property. They want the drainage ditch moved so that they can build a pool, but the city says that the apartment complex can keep their drainage ditch where it is because it was built when their property was just an empty lot, giving the apartment complex what is called a "prescriptive easement." How would you feel if you were 1) Marcie Brown, 2) the owner of the apartment complex, 3) Marcie Brown's kids (who probably won't get a pool)?

3. Your city plans to demolish several blocks of old hotels and low-income apartment houses to build a new baseball stadium. Several hundred people will lose their homes. While the owners of the buildings will be paid by the city, the renters won't get anything. They band together and try to stop the city from building the ballpark. How would you feel if you were 1) a renter in danger of losing your home, 2) the owner of one of the condemned buildings, 3) the developer of the baseball stadium, 4) the city mayor, 5) a baseball fan?

4. Kim and Tracey have been best friends for years. One day Susan moves in next door to Kim and the two girls quickly become inseparable. Tracey tries to make it a threesome, but finds herself left out much of the time. How would you feel if you were 1) Tracey, 2) Kim, 3) Susan?

5. Jermane spends hours in the library researching the Lewis and Clark expedition for a written report. He gets a B. His friend Donovan downloads a report from the Internet and gets an A. Jermane complains to his mom who, against Jermane's wishes, tells the teacher. How would you feel if you were 1) Jermane, 2) Jermane's mother, 3) the teacher, 4) Donovan?

Give a copy of the experience sheet, "Empathy Practice," to each student. Go over the directions. Announce that for one week, you want them to watch and listen for feelings. Point out that feelings are a lot more difficult to notice than physical things like how someone looks. Suggest that the students be alert for situations that involve some sort of problem or conflict, like the ones you read to them earlier.

When the students bring in their completed sheets, have them take turns reporting what they observed. Go around the group and discuss one situation from each student. Then repeat the circuit as time allows.

Discussion Questions

1. *What is the most difficult thing about being empathetic?*
2. *What kinds of feelings were easier to discern, positive feelings or negative feelings? Why do you think that is?*
3. *Why is having empathy important?*
4. *Would you rather have friends who empathize with what you feel, or friends who don't seem to notice? Why?*

Empathy Is...

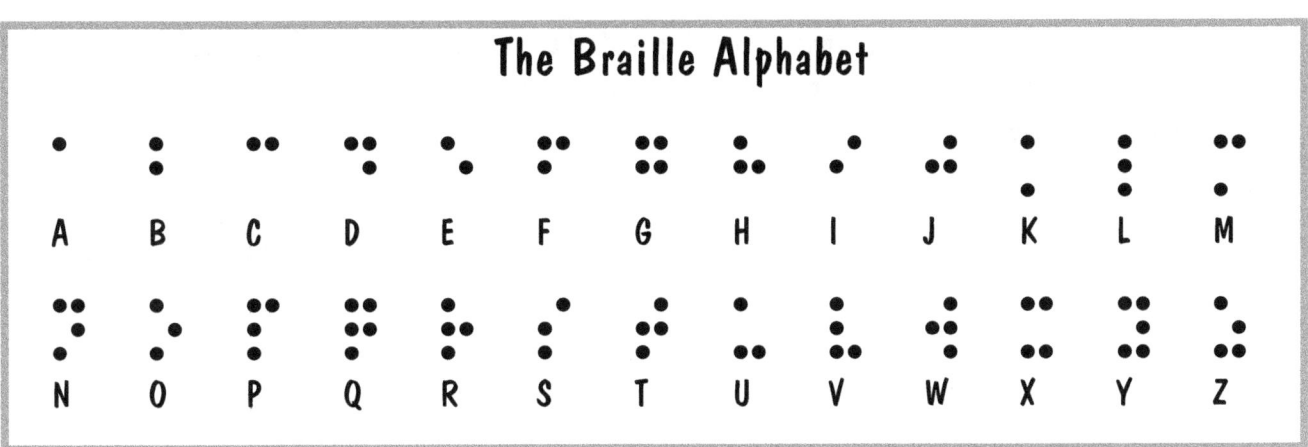

Using the Braille alphabet above, translate the following sentence. (Each word is separately underlined.)

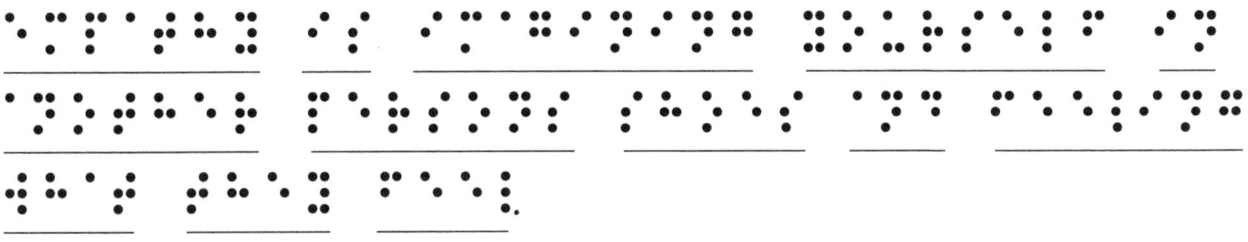

Write your translation here:

_____

_____

_____

_____

_____

_____

_____

Empathy Practice

For one week, notice situations in which people have strong feelings. Write down what was going on. Then try to empathize with each of the people involved. Write down what you think they feel.

Situation:	Feelings

Responsible and Dependable

I believe that every right implies a responsibility; every opportunity an obligation; every possession a duty.
—JOHN D. ROCKEFELLER, JR.

Objectives

The students will:
1. Explain the meaning of dependability.
2. Describe how one person's lack of dependability affects others in typical situations.
3. Identify people they depend on for specific things.
4. Describe how people can depend on them.

Materials

One copy of the experience sheet, "I Depend on You—You Depend on Me," for each student

Procedure

Begin by defining and discussing the word *responsible*. Explore various meanings of the term. For example, ask:

— *When someone tells you, "This is your responsibility," what does that mean?*
— *What does it mean to be a responsible person?*
— *How do you feel when someone praises you for being a responsible person?*
— *How do you become a responsible person?*

Read the following scenarios to the students and ask the accompanying questions. Encourage the students to think of all the people who might be affected in each story, and how they would be affected (consequences).

- Sally has a lead role in the school play. Practices are on Monday and Wednesday evenings. Sally is playing with a friend one Monday afternoon and loses track of time. She misses a rehearsal.

— *Who are the people affected by Sally's absence? How are they affected?*
— *Do you think the other actors and the director will want to depend on Sally in the future? Why or why not?*

- Six people plan a surprise birthday party for one of their friends. They figure out a menu and everyone agrees to bring one dish. Tom is supposed to bring a decorated birthday cake from the bakery, but he forgets to order it. An hour before the party he rushes down to the supermarket and buys a ready-made cake with no decorations.

  — *Who is affected and how?*
  — *If you were one of Tom's friends, would you want to depend on him for future events? Why or why not?*

- Three students are working together on a project for the science fair. On the day of the fair, two agree to come to the auditorium early and set up the display. The third, Lila, agrees to make a chart outlining the steps in the group's experiment. Lila buys only one piece of poster board, and then puts off making the chart until late the night before. When she messes it up, she has to wait until the next morning to get more poster board and redo the chart. By the time she gets to the auditorium, the judges have already passed her group's display.

  — *Who is affected and how?*
  — *What could Lila have done differently?*

Distribute the experience sheets. Instruct the students to list people they can always depend on, and describe what they depend on them for. In addition, tell the students to describe one thing each of the people listed can depend on them (the students) to do.

Have the students share their experience sheets in groups of three to five. Lead a follow-up discussion.

Discussion Questions

1. *Are you sometimes responsible for a younger brother or sister? What are your parents depending on you to do?*
2. *How do we depend on each other here in class?*
3. *What are some ways in which people in a community depend on one another?*
4. *Does being dependable mean you can never make a mistake? Explain.*
5. *What would the world be like if we could never depend on others?*

I Depend on You—You Depend on Me

Responsible people are people you can depend on. They keep their promises. They do their best, even when it is hard. They do their duty to others, to the community, and to the country.

Think of people you can always depend on. Describe one thing you depend on each person to do. Then describe one thing each person can depend on you to do.

People I Depend On

Name	I can always depend on this person for...	This person can always depend on me for...

Who Is Responsible?

You cannot dream yourself into a character; you must hammer and forge yourself one.
—JAMES A. FROUDE

Objectives

The students will:
1. Make decisions about who is responsible in specific situations.
2. Describe alternative responsible behaviors.

Materials

One copy of the experience sheet, "Who Is Responsible?," for each student, (optional) a copy of *The Book of Virtues: A Treasury of Great Moral Stories**.

Procedure

Begin this activity by announcing to the students that you have one or two stories to read (or tell) them, or you may choose to have the students do a group reading. Two excellent stories are summarized on the following pages. The original versions of both are printed in *The Book of Virtues*.

After reading (or telling) the stories, engage the students in a discussion concerning who was, or should have been, responsible for what. Help the students recognize three moral lessons illustrated in the stories:

1. People are obligated to care for each other and their animals.
2. Parents are responsible for guiding their children.
3. Children have a responsibility to listen to, and follow, their parents' guidance.

Distribute the experience sheets. Have a volunteer read each scenario aloud while the rest of the group follows along. Answer the questions as a group, discussing the opinions and views of students.

Conclude the activity with more questions and a summary discussion.

Discussion Questions

1. *Imagine that you are the little kid having rocks thrown at him in the first scenario, or the person who lost the wallet in the second scenario, or the dog in the third scenario. How would you feel if no one were responsible enough to care about you or help you?*
2. *Is it always a good idea to help someone who is asking for help? Is helping always the most responsible thing to do?*
3. *How can you tell if a situation is your responsibility?*
4. *Why is it important to know who is responsible for what?*

Variations

Have volunteers role play the scenarios, trying out various responsible behaviors. Facilitate discussion.

Tell primary-age children the tale, "The Boy Who Cried Wolf." Then ask them questions tailored to your version. Here are samples:

— *What did the boy do that was not responsible?*
— *Why did all the sheep finally get eaten by the wolves?*
— *If you had been one of the people who lived in the village, would you have believed the boy after he cried wolf the first two times?*
— *Today we don't have villages and sheep like the people in the story, but the boy had been given an important job to do. It was his responsibility. Do you think children today can help with important jobs and be responsible?*

From the scenarios, choose examples that younger children can readily relate to. After reading them aloud, ask the children to describe responsible actions in those situations.

*Bennett, William J. (Ed.). (1993). *The book of virtues: A Treasury of Great Moral Stories*. New York: Simon and Schuster.

The Bell of Atri

The king installed a bell in a tower in the Italian town of Atri, and announced to the people that the bell should only be rung when someone felt he or she had been wronged. Through the years, every time the bell was rung, the judges came together to right each wrong. After years of wear and tear, the bell's rope became old, torn, and shortened. This worried the judges, because if a child were wronged, the child would not be able to reach the rope. To solve this problem, a man tied a grapevine to the end of the rope, making it long and strong enough for even the smallest child to operate.

In the hills above Atri lived a man who had been a famous knight when he was younger. He had a great horse who was his best friend and had saved him from many dangers in his knighthood days. But as the man grew older, he became a miser and loved nothing but gold. He sold everything he could for money except his horse, which had grown very old and feeble. The man thought no one wanted the horse, so he turned it out without trying to sell it. The poor horse could barely find enough grass to eat and was slowly starving and freezing from the cold. People ran the horse off and treated it badly.

One day, shortly after the grapevine was tied to the rope of the bell of Atri, the horse was looking for food and wandered near the tower. The horse saw the green leaves on the grapevine and took a bite, which pulled the rope. The bell sounded, and it seemed to say, "Someone has done me wrong!" The judges came running and immediately saw the situation: The poor horse was telling the world how it felt in the best way it could. They ordered the old miserly knight brought before them and made him spend half of his gold on food, a new stable, and a green pasture for his poor old horse.

Icarus and Daedalus

Daedalus was a very famous and clever builder and artist in ancient Greece. King Minos of the nearby island of Crete had a big problem: A minotaur (a horrible monster that was half bull, half man) was on the loose. Minos succeeded in getting Daedalus to come to Crete to build a prison that would hold the beast. Icarus, the young son of Daedalus, went with his father. Daedalus designed and built the prison, but when he and his son wanted to sail back to Greece, Minor imprisoned them in the top of a tower. He wanted Daedalus to be on call to take care of any other problems that might arise.

Being very clever and never giving up, Daedalus came up with a method of escape, which he learned from the sea gulls as he watched them fly. After collecting lots of feathers, he created a huge pair of wings fastened together with string and wax. Then he taught himself to use them. Next, Daedalus made a pair for Icarus, and gave his son flying lessons. Then Daedalus and Icarus waited for the perfect day when the winds would be just right for flying back home to Greece.

When the right day came, father and son prepared to leave, but first Daedalus gave Icarus a warning: "Don't fly too low, because the sea spray will get your wings wet and bog them down, or too high, because the sun's rays will melt the wax. Either way you'll crash. Just stay by me and you'll be fine." As they took off, both were scared, but soon they got used to flying and Icarus in particular became full of joy. He forgot his father's warning and sailed higher and higher.

Daedalus yelled for his son to come back, but Icarus was completely overcome with the urge to get as close to the heavens as he could. Little by little the feathers came off, then all of a sudden the wax melted completely, and no matter how much he beat his arms up and down Icarus could not stay aloft; he fell into the sea and drowned. Daedalus, a sad father, finally found his son's body and carried it to Greece for burial. Later he built a temple over the grave in memory of the son he loved so much, who failed to follow his guidance at a crucial time.

Who Is Responsible

Scenario 1
You and your parents are visiting the home of some friends. One of the boys in the family, who is your age, throws a rock at his little brother. No adults are around at the time.
—Do you have a responsibility to do anything?
—If so, what is the most responsible thing to do?

Scenario 2
You enter a store with one of your parents, and see a wallet on the floor. You pick up the wallet and look inside. You see that the wallet contains money. Your parent has not noticed any of this.
—Do you have a responsibility to do anything?
—If so, what is the most responsible thing to do?

Scenario 3
Your sister begged for a puppy for her birthday and got one. But now, almost a year later, she has practically forgotten the dog. She rarely gives him fresh water, or feeds, or plays with him.
—What is the most responsible thing to do in this situation?

Scenario 4
Your friend comes up to you before school starts and tells you she didn't do her homework and wants to copy yours.
—Who is responsible for your friend's homework?
—What is the best thing for you to do?

Scenario 5
Your friend is angry at his sister and his dad. Yesterday he got into a fight with his sister, which he says was all her fault, but his dad punished them both. Today you are at your friend's house and you are thinking about what happened.
—Do you have any responsibilities in this situation?

Caring in the News

We are shaped and fashioned by what we love.
—GOETHE

Objectives

The students will:
1. Identify news reports featuring the caring actions of citizens.
2. Acknowledge specific individuals for performing caring, helpful acts.

Materials

Sources of human-interest stories such as newspapers, Reader's Digest, *Chicken Soup For The Soul* books, or stories found at the web site www.heroicstories.com; writing materials

Procedure

Share a story about a person who did something that demonstrated caring. Explain that much of what we read in the newspapers or see on television newscasts is negative. We see people breaking the law or doing things to hurt other people. Emphasize that many people do good things that help other people. Refer to the example of your story, or tell about events you know of in which people have performed helpful, caring deeds. Cite examples of people who have helped others in natural disasters, such as earthquakes, floods, hurricanes, and the 9/11 terrorist attack. Tell about people who have made breakthroughs in the medical field or invented things that helped humanity.

Ask the students to look through newspapers and other sources and identify articles that feature people who have performed good deeds. Those who enjoy writing can transcribe stories from TV newscasts, and then write up their own accounts in feature articles. As an alternative, have the students write about caring actions they see in the classroom or throughout the school.

After each student shares his or her news story, encourage contemplation by asking some of the discussion questions listed below.

Post the stories on a bulletin board under the heading, "Caring in the News."

After a variety of news stories have been collected and shared, ask the students to choose one person (or group) who performed a caring act and write letters to that person. Invite the students to praise the person for his or her actions and thank the person for contributing to the world, the nation, the community, the school, or the classroom.

Address the letters to the individual in care of the newspaper or magazine in which the article was published, or the television station from which the news was broadcast.

Conclude the activity with a summary discussion.

Discussion Questions

1. What was the caring act in this news story?
2. How would things have been different if the person hadn't performed the caring or helpful act?
3. Was the caring act spontaneous or did the person plan it in advance?
4. Was this the sort of thing that anybody could do, or did it take special training?
5. Why is it important to thank people who perform caring acts?
6. How would the school, community, nation, or world be different if we all did caring deeds every day?

Variations

In primary classrooms, read several news events and ask the class to select one. Have the children dictate a class thank-you letter while you record it on large paper. Ask the children to sign their names to the letter. Enclose drawings depicting the students' interpretations of the caring deed.

Make this activity a year-long project in which students write notes of praise and thanks each month to various caring people.

Taking Control of Anger

There's only one corner of the universe you can be certain of improving; and that's your own self.
—ALDOUS HUXLEY

Objectives

The students will:
1. Brainstorm strategies for managing anger.
2. Select and think through six preferred anger management strategies.

Materials

One experience sheet, "Six Strategies for Controlling Anger," for each student; scissors, tape, pencils, crayons, colored markers; colored construction paper precut to form cards 3-1/2 x 5 inches in size.

Procedure

Ask the students to think about a time that they were really mad and yet were able to calm down and get their anger under control. Ask:

—*What helped you to calm down?*

On the board or chart paper, record the calming strategies suggested by the students. If they are not mentioned, add the following:

- Take several deep breaths.
- Count to 10.
- Distract yourself by doing something fun.
- Share your feelings with an adult or friend you trust.
- Do something active like ride a bike, hit a baseball or tennis ball, jog, or dance.
- Imagine a peaceful place.
- Quietly talk to yourself until you calm down.
- Write down both sides of the problem and think it through.
- Listen to your favorite music.
- Physically remove yourself from the situation. Walk away.
- Remind yourself of the consequences of out-of-control anger.

Distribute the experience sheets. Have the students choose their top six strategies of managing anger and illustrate them in the squares on the experience sheet. Suggest that they choose from the brainstormed list, and add other ideas as well. Provide pencils, crayons and markers.

Distribute scissors, construction paper cards and glue. Have the students cut out their illustrated strategies and glue them to construction paper cards, leaving a boarder all the way around.

Have the children take turns sharing their cards. Use some of the discussion questions to stimulate discussion during the sharing period.

Discussion Questions

1. *In what kinds of situations will this strategy work best?*
2. *How well has this strategy worked when you've used it before?*
3. *What kinds of things cause kids to get angry?*
4. *What kinds of things provoke anger in adults?*
5. *What happens when anger gets out of control?*
6. *What are some examples of justifiable anger?*
7. *When anger is justifiable, is it less threatening? Why or why not?*

Variations

When everyone has had a turn sharing, give the students a few minutes to mingle and negotiate trades.

Six Strategies for Controlling Anger

In the six boxes, illustrate and label your top six strategies for calming down when you are angry. Use symbols and drawings.

#1	#2
#3	#4
#5	#6

When It's Right to Say No

What we become depends not on conditions but on decisions.
—Hal Urban
Life's Greatest Lessons

Objectives

The students will:
1. Identify specific reasons why people have trouble saying no.
2. Describe a situation in which they had difficulty saying no.
3. Learn effective methods for saying no.
5. Practice saying no by role playing actual situations.

Materials

Copies of the experience sheet "The Cool Kid's Guide to Saying No" (recommended for younger students), or "The Smart Student's Guide to Saying No" (for more mature students)

Procedure

Begin by asking the students why they think people—adults and kids alike—so often have difficulty saying "no" to others when they want them to do something they don't want to do or know they shouldn't do. If the students have trouble answering this question, ask them to think about their own experiences. Here are some possible reasons:

- Children are taught to obey their parents and other authority figures. Sometimes they are punished for not obeying.
- We learn through experience that saying no sometimes causes the other person to feel disappointed, rejected, unhappy, or even angry.
- Most of us learn that it is socially acceptable to conform, do what we're told, and not make waves.
- Most of us—young people especially—want to fit in and be accepted by our peers. We accomplish this by going along with the crowd—in effect, saying yes.

Point out that in the aftermath of all this learning and training, we end up doing things that we don't want to do and probably shouldn't do. We may even by tempted to do things that we know are illegal or dangerous.

Ask the students, "What's the answer to this dilemma?" Through discussion, help them to arrive at the conclusion that they must learn new ways of responding that help them to:

— stay out of trouble
— make legal, safe choices
— say no without losing friends

Explain that this lesson is about saying no *skillfully*, using methods that put you in control of a situation. In the process, you think through the situation and make a conscious decision.

Distribute the appropriate experience sheet. Read through the steps with the students, answering questions and facilitating discussion.

Next, ask the students to think of a situation in which they had a hard time saying no. Instruct them to write a description of the situation on a slip of paper. Caution them not to use names.

Collect the papers.

Read one of the situations to the group. One at a time, go through the steps outlined on the experience sheet, explaining how each skill can be used in that situation. Ask two students to role play the situation in front of the group. Coach the students, as needed.

Read a second situation. This time ask the *students* to explain how each step can be used. Again, ask volunteers to role play the situation. Repeat this process with as many more situations as you have time for. Then lead a culminating discussion.

Discussion Questions

1. *Why would you want to keep a friend who asks you to do something you shouldn't do?*
2. *Have you ever succeeded in saying no without making the other person unhappy or angry? How did you do it?*
3. *How does it feel to stay in control of a difficult situation?*
4. *How does it feel to get pulled along in a situation you don't want to be part of?*
5. *What is the hardest part about saying no?*
6. *Which steps in the process do you most need to work on?*
7. *Why is it important to avoid arguing and debating?*
8. *In what kinds of situations would you want to "keep the door open?" When would this not matter to you at all?*
9. *What kind of body language is most helpful in situations like these?*
10. *How can you be sure that you will recall these steps when actually facing a situation?*

The Cool Kid's Guide to Saying No

What can you say when someone tries to get you to do something you don't want to do? How should you respond when someone asks you to take part in something that is illegal or dangerous? Here are some helpful guidelines.

1. Say no.
Say it clearly, flatly and confidently. Be assertive. When someone pressures you in a friendly way, remember that you can be friendly too—even humorous—and be assertive at the same time.

2. Say no and give a reason.
Briefly state why you are not going to do whatever the person is suggesting. Use appropriate voice and body language. Let your facial expression show calm confidence. Speak clearly, in a firm, steady voice.

3. Say no and suggest something else to do.
There are lots of ways to have fun. Think of something you both enjoy that is safe and legal. Suggest it, but don't get into a debate.

4. Say no and leave.
Don't waste your time arguing with the person. If steps 1-3 haven't worked, walk away. If you are threatened, skip steps 1-3 and leave immediately.

The Smart Student's Guide to Saying No

Sometimes people ask you to do things that you're not sure about. Trust your instincts. If you have even the slightest doubt, find out what's really going on. You can gain control of yourself and the situation by following these steps:

1. Get information.
If you have any doubts about whether the activity means trouble, ask questions. "Who's going?" "What do you plan to do?" "What will happen then?" "Is it safe?" "Do your parents know about this?" By asking questions, you get everyone to think the situation through. This helps you (and everyone else) gain control.

2. Name the trouble.
As soon as you recognize trouble, put a label on it. "That's stealing." "That's illegal." "That's a lie." Say it clearly and assertively so no one can pretend ignorance.

3. Describe the consequences.
Think about and describe what could happen. Make sure the others understand the risks they are about to take. "You could be arrested." "Your parents will be furious." "That stuff can kill you."

4. Suggest alternatives.
There are many ways to have a good time. Think of something enjoyable that is also safe and legal. "Why don't we all go over to my house instead." "Let's go shoot some baskets." "How about a pizza."

5. Leave.
If your suggestions don't work, just leave. Arguing and debating are a waste of time and seldom produce results.

6. Keep the door open.
One of the goals of refusal skills is to keep your friends. If that's important to you, try not to judge or condemn anyone. Leave, but leave the door open to future contact. "Okay, I'm going to shoot some baskets. Join me later if you change your mind."

We're All Different - and the Same

All the people like us are "we" and everyone else is "they."
RUDYARD KIPLING

Objectives:

The Students Will:
1. Identify ways we are all different, and the same.
2. Identify differences and similarities between themselves and another student.
3. Describe benefits that result from accepting differences and recognizing similarities.

Materials:

A copy of the Experience Sheet " Five Things We All Like" for each team.

Procedure:

Discuss some of the many ways in which people are different. On the board write terms such as; race, religion, gender, handicap, ethnicity, economic level, place of residence, education, and values. Discuss the meaning of each. (Select terms that are relevant to the level of understanding of your children). Point out that these are some of the major ways in which people are different. Ask the students:

- How do people generally react to these difference in others?
- How do you feel when you are with someone who is different from you?
- How do you feel when you are with someone who is the same?

Next, ask the students to form pairs. Tell them to turn toward each other. Say: *Look at your partner and notice as many things as you can about your partner that are different from you.* (If need be provide a few ideas such as eye color, length of hair, number of family members etc.). *Take turns and tell each other two things you notice that are different.* Once the students have done that, ask them to notice things that are the same. Allow a few minutes for them to share two similarities they notice with each other. Once each student has had a chance to share in their team ask the teams to take turns sharing with the entire group the differences and similarities they noticed.

When the teams have finished sharing similarities and differences with the entire group have the pairs team up to form groups of four. Pass out a copy of the Experience Sheet "Five Things We All Like" to each group along with a writing implement. Ask each group member to sign their name at the top of the Experience Sheet where indicated. Also ask each group to select a recorder. Next, instruct the teams to talk among themselves to discover, and record, five things that they ALL like in common. For example, if all four members like puppies then puppies could be one of the items they list. But, if three team members like chocolate ice cream but one doesn't then chocolate ice cream can't be put on their list.

Circulate and help out where needed, perhaps by offering categories to select from. Allow time for the students to talk and share as the process of finding commonality is an important one.

When all the teams have completed their Experience Sheets have them take turns sharing their likes with the entire class. Culminate by leading a group discussion on what they have learned from this activity.

Discussion Questions:

1. *Do we all have things in common?*
2. *Are our commonalities as important as our differences?*
3. *Is it important to understand how we are different?*
4. *Is it important to understand how we are the same?*
5. *How would the world be different if people could accept each others differences?*
6. *How would the world be different if people could understand how we are all the same in many ways?*

Five Things We All Like

Our team members are —

1. _____ 2. _____

3. _____ 4. _____

1. _____

2. _____

3. _____

4. _____

5. _____

No Room for Stereotypes

Our lives begin to end the day we become silent about things that matter.
—MARTIN LUTHER KING JR.

Objectives

The students will:
1. Understand the nature of prejudice and stereotyping.
2. Develop strategies for being tolerant of differences.

Materials

The experience sheet, "Shattering Stereotypes," for each student

Procedure

Ask the students if they know what *stereotype* means. What *prejudice* means. Come up with a class understanding of both words. Use the dictionary if necessary. Write the agreed upon definitions on the board.

Point out that prejudice often begins with a bad experience that is generalized into a stereotype. Explain this concept by having the students think of a person who is different from themselves with whom they had a bad experience. The difference doesn't need to be ethnic or racial, and the person could be anyone—a dentist, doctor, police officer, teacher, big kid, etc. Ask volunteers to share some of their experiences, but ask them not to share names. Share an example of your own, as well. As they share, ask, "Did your bad experience develop into a prejudice? Why or why not?"

Distribute Part 1 of the experience sheet, "Shattering Stereotypes." Ask the students to complete each line with the first thing that comes to mind. Ask them not to stop and think, but just to write their responses. Point out that stereotypes are not always negative—they can sometimes be positive.

Give the students a couple of minutes to complete this first part of the experience sheet. Then ask them to share some of their responses. Encourage discussion by asking some of the discussion questions.

Pass out Part 2 of the experience sheet. Direct the students' attention to the dot pattern. Explain that this is a puzzle. Tell them to use a pencil to join all nine dots with four straight lines, without lifting their pencils or retracing any lines. After the students have had a minute or two to try various solutions, ask if anyone solved the puzzle. Ask a successful student to demonstrate the solution on the board. If no one succeeded, demonstrate it yourself.

This is accomplished by beginning at Point A, drawing a line to point B, continuing on to point C, returning to point A, and finishing by going to point D.

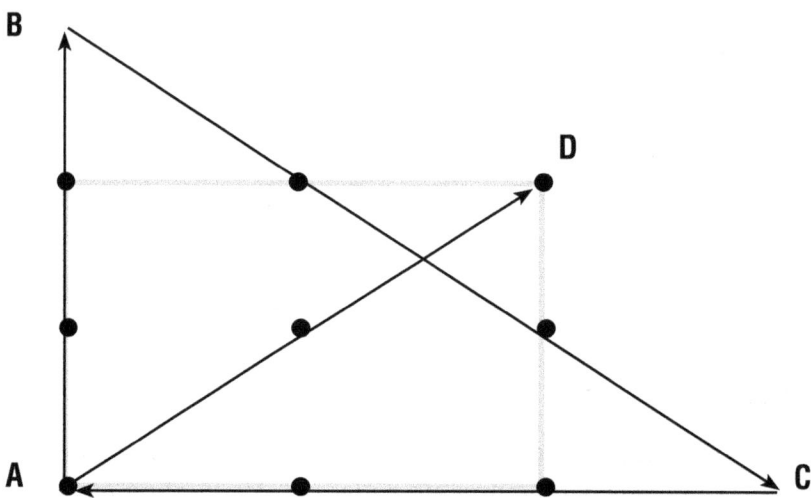

Point out that most of us find the puzzle difficult because we refuse to go outside the "box" created by the nine dots. Based on our prior experiences and beliefs, our brains interpret the nine dots as a box, and we assume that the lines will form a box also. Figuratively speaking, we are "boxed in" by our previous experience.

Encourage the students to relate this experience to the stereotypes they listed in Part 1 of the experience sheet. Use the discussion questions to stimulate thought.

Discussion Questions

1. *Where do you think you learned the stereotyped ideas you wrote down?*
2. *Which stereotypes bother you most?*
3. *How do stereotypes perpetuate prejudice?*
4. *What can we do to eliminate stereotypes?*
5. *How do stereotypes work to "box you in?"*
6. *How does being boxed in cheat you?*

Shattering Stereotypes

Part 1

Write down your first reaction to each statement. Don't take time to think about it—just write.

- Indians all/always _____.
- Mexicans all/always _____.
- Football players all/always _____.
- Blondes all/always _____.
- Texans all/always _____.
- Skinheads all/always _____.
- Blacks all/always _____.
- Italians all/always _____.
- Arabs all/always _____.
- Teachers all/always _____.
- Teens all/always _____.
- Boys all/always _____.
- Girls all/always _____.
- Old people all/always _____.
- Police all/always _____.
- Whites all/always _____.
- Americans all/always _____.
- Hollywood stars all/always _____.
- Millionaires all/always _____.
- Politicians all/always _____.

Part 2

Connect all nine dots using only four straight lines. Do not lift your pencil from the paper. Do not retrace any lines.

Fighting Prejudice, Stereotypes and Discrimination

All we can know for certain is our own intent. Intent is everything in determining morality. Good intentions are not always enough but without them we have nothing.
—*Vincent Rush*

Objectives

The students will:
1. Identify dangers of apathy in the face of prejudice.
2. Develop guidelines for speaking up against prejudice.

Materials

Writing materials for the students; marking pens; several sheets of poster paper or poster board for the final chart

Procedure

In your own words, say to the students:

Racism is a serious problem in many schools today. Our school is no exception. At times you may have witnessed name-calling, slurs, threats, or even fights. In some schools racial hate groups spend their time harassing and terrorizing minority students. Racism hurts everyone. It promotes stereotypes and prevents people from really getting to know one another. It can have a terrible effect on a person's self-worth and self-esteem.

Ask:

—*What are some acts of racism, prejudice or discrimination that you have witnessed here at school or elsewhere?*
—*How could these incidents have been prevented?*

Facilitate discussion, cautioning the students not to identify people by name.

As a total group, brainstorm some of the factors involved in overt and covert racism and intolerance. Write all ideas on the board. The students will need this list later while working in small groups. Try to elicit these and other ideas:

- Instead of objecting to racist remarks, people often ignore them. Some students snicker or laugh at racist jokes instead of saying "That's not funny."
- Acts of discrimination and favoritism (for example, when most awards or elected offices go to the students of one race) often go unnoticed and unchallenged. Vigilance and activism are needed to stem such practices.
- Kids tend to hang out with other kids who are like them, racially and in other ways. Reaching out to and befriending students from other groups promotes understanding and is personally rewarding.
- People are quick to label normal conflicts between individuals as "racially motivated" when in fact they are no different from conflicts between people of the same race. This retards communication and makes it difficult to resolve differences productively.
- People are afraid to talk about their racist feelings. We all have prejudices. Instead of pretending we don't, or ignoring them, we need to get them out in the open and discuss them.

Have the students form small groups of 6 to 8. Tell them that you want each group to brainstorm strategies that the entire student body can use to promote tolerance and diversity. Have each group appoint a recorder to write down all ideas, using the group list just created as a springboard. Suggest that each strategy begin with an "action word" that says what the individual student must do to carry out the strategy. Examples of action words are: *work, reach out, stand up, promote, accept, speak up, learn, talk to, join*.

Allow at least 15 minutes for brainstorming. Circulate and offer encouragement as needed. Then have each group read its ideas to the rest of the class. Using the discussion questions below, facilitate discussion.

Have a team of two or three volunteers compile all of the strategies into a single list, combining similar items. Then, at a later session, work with the class to reduce the list to no more than 10 strategies. Be sure each of the final strategies is worded clearly and includes examples of specific behaviors. Have the same (or a different) team of volunteers make the final chart or poster. Display it in the classroom and elsewhere in the school.

Discussion Questions

1. *Why is it important to fight racism actively and openly?*
2. *Why do so many people ignore racist remarks, jokes and behaviors?*
3. *What impression does a racist person get when his or her remarks and actions are tolerated by others?*
4. *What can you do to help promote tolerance and diversity?*

Nonviolent Communication

Contention does not profit a people.
—BRIGHAM YOUNG

Objectives

The students will:
1. Practice Nonviolent Communication (NVC) to resolve conflict.
2. Contrast NVC statements with demanding, threatening statements usually used in conflict.
3. Recognize that NVC Communication helps develop mutual compassion.

Materials

One copy of the experience sheet, "Settle Your Differences with Nonviolent Communication," for each student

Procedure

Announce that in this session the group is going to look at a special way of resolving conflict—through Nonviolent Communication*

Ask the students to describe what usually happens in conflict. Write some of their ideas on the board. They will probably suggest that people argue, fight, yell, hit, cry, call each other names, try to get what they want, etc.

If you have already led the activity, "Heart Power," remind the students of some of the things they learned about compassion. If not, write the word *compassion* on the board and ask the students what it means. Record their ideas. Have a student check the dictionary and read the definition to the group. The following definition is from the American Heritage Dictionary:

A deep awareness of the suffering of another coupled with a wish to relieve it.

Ask:

—Isn't that what most of us want in a conflict? Aren't we trying to get the other person to understand our suffering and be willing to relieve it?

Explain that with the Nonviolent Communication approach, that is exactly what happens. People develop compassion for each other's feelings, needs and point of view. Point out that only reasonably calm people can use this process, so before starting, both (or all) of those involved in the conflict must take time to calm down.

Review the Nonviolent Communications model. Write the following headings on the board:

1. Observation
2. Feelings
3. Needs
4. Request

Explain that Nonviolent Communication involves an awareness of these four components. Explain the components as follows:

1. Observation

First you need to describe what is actually happening in the situation. What is the other person saying or doing that is interfering with your needs? The trick is to be able to describe this observation without blaming or judging—to simply say what the other person is doing that you don't like.

Example: *Anna, the marking pens were left open all night.*

2. Feelings

Second, state how you feel when you observe this behavior. Are you hurt? Scared? Joyful? Amused? Irritated? Frustrated? Jealous?

Example: *Anna, the marking pens were left open all night. When I see this I feel worried that they will dry up and soon we won't have any marking pens.*

3. Needs

Third, describe what you need. The need is connected to your feelings.

Example: *Anna, the marking pens were left open all night. When I see this I feel worried that soon they will dry up and soon we won't have any marking pens. I need to know that they are covered at night so they won't dry out.*

4. Request

Fourth, ask for what you want from the other person. Be specific.

Example: *Anna, the marking pens were left open all night. When I see this I feel worried that they will dry up and soon we won't have any marking pens. I need to know that they are covered at night so they won't dry out. Will you remember to put the caps on them after you use them?*

Explain that after the students have expressed the four pieces of information very clearly, they should be ready to receive the same four pieces of information from the other person. This allows them to find out what the other person is observing, feeling, needing and requesting *of them*.

Stress that through this flow of statements, back and forth, what each person is observing, feeling, needing and requesting gradually becomes clear. In the process, both people develop compassion for the other person's experience.

Distribute the experience sheets. Go over the directions with the students. Allow a few minutes for the students to complete the experience sheet.

Ask two volunteers to act out the first "violent" response and then each of their nonviolent responses. Contrast the two efforts and discuss their effectiveness. Then invite other students to come forward, step into the role play and substitute their own nonviolent statements. Repeat the process with the second violent statement on the experience sheet.

Discussion Questions

(Ask after each role play.)

1. *What need was expressed in this statement?*
2. *Do you feel empathy or compassion for this person? Why or why not?*
3. *Could the request have been clearer? How?*

(Ask at any time during the activity to stimulate discussion.)

1. *What information do you need in order to feel compassion for someone?*
2. *Why do people have so much trouble resolving conflicts?*
3. *Why is it difficult to think about the other person's needs in a conflict?*
4. *Why is it important to calm down before trying to use the nonviolent approach?*
5. *What should you do if either you or the other person hasn't calmed down?*
6. *When do you need to ask a third person to help resolve a conflict? Who could you ask?*

*Rosenberg, M. (2003). *Nonviolent Communications: A Language of Life.* Encinitas, CA: PuddleDancer Press. Adapted with permission. *For more information visit www.cnvc.org and www.nonviolentcommunication.com.*

Settle Your Differences with Nonviolent Communication

When another person does something that interferes with your needs, you may be tempted to make accusations, demands or threats. These are "violent" messages. They can make the other person feel angry or hurt, and can make the situation worse.

Try using Nonviolent Communication (NVC). Describe your observations, feelings and needs. This will help the other person understand where you are coming from. When the other person understands, he or she will probably feel compassion for your situation and want to help. This will make the situation better.

Here's how to use NVC:

1. **Observe and state what is happening.**
   "You've been on the phone for an hour..."

2. **State how you feel about what is happening.**
   "...and I'm getting worried..."

3. **Describe what you need.**
   "...because I need to leave for soccer practice."

4. **Make a specific request.**
   "Can you please make the rest of your calls later so we can go?"

Here's another example. Look at the difference.

Violent:
"You sneak! You took my bike without asking. Touch it again, I'll knock your head off."

Nonviolent:
"My bike is gone. I feel really scared, because I need to know that it's in a safe place when I'm not using it. I want you to ask before using my bike, and always put it back where it belongs."

Now, you try it. Read the violent statement in the first cartoon bubble. Then write a nonviolent statement in the second bubble.

Cartoon 1.

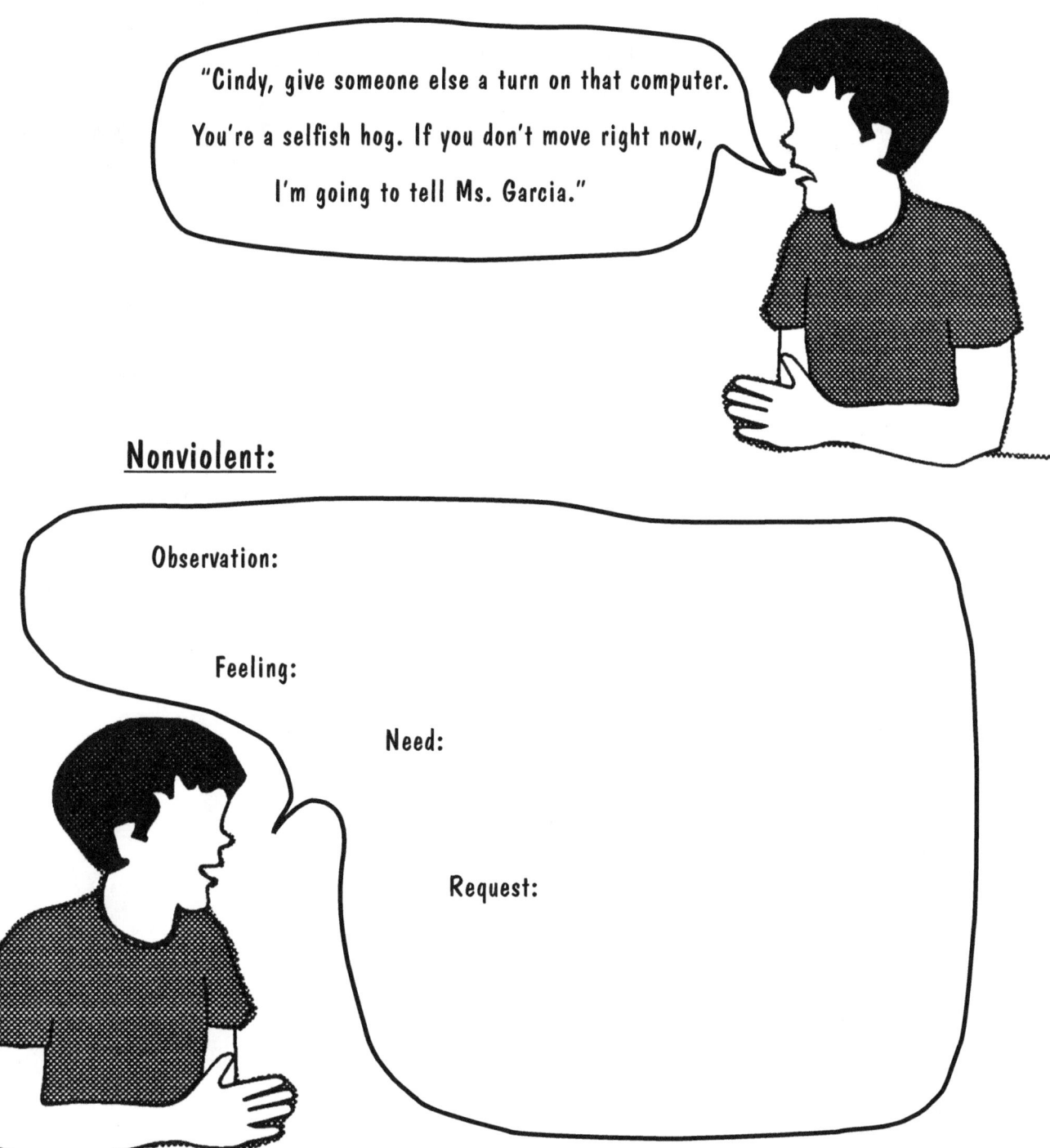

"Cindy, give someone else a turn on that computer. You're a selfish hog. If you don't move right now, I'm going to tell Ms. Garcia."

Nonviolent:

Observation:

Feeling:

Need:

Request:

Cartoon 2.

Win-Win Role Play

*There are always two sides to a conflict.
It's just that we usually can't see one from the other.*
—DAVID COWAN

Objectives

The students will:
1. Role-play interpersonal conflicts.
2. Generate possible solutions to the conflicts.
3. Evaluate and choose solutions using "win-win" guidelines.

Materials

One copy of the experience sheet, "How to Create Win-Win Solutions to Conflict," for each students

Procedure

Have the students sit in a circle. Explain that the group will be focusing on personal conflicts and brainstorming solutions to those conflicts.

Invite volunteers to share a recent conflict with the group. Explain that they can tell about a conflict with another student or an adult, a conflict that occurred at school, at home, during baseball or soccer practice, or just about anywhere else. Caution the students not to identify the other people in the conflict by name.

Listen to several conflicts. Find out how each one was resolved and how the person felt about it.

Choose one conflict to role play. Pick one that was not satisfactorily resolved. Allow the person whose conflict was selected to play him or herself and to choose one or more classmates to play the parts of the other people involved. Have the players act out the conflict exactly as it occurred.

Encourage the group to analyze what happened—how each person seemed to feel, what was done about the conflict, who won and who lost.

Distribute the experience sheet. Go over the guidelines for arriving at a win-win solution.

Now, replay the conflict, following the first three (3) steps on the experience sheet. Coach the actors through this process.

Stop the action when you get to step 4 (the brainstorming step). Lead the entire group in brainstorming possible solutions while you write them on the board. Involve the group in evaluating the suggested solutions as well. Allow the actors to make the final choice. Continue coaching them through the commitment step.

Repeat this process with additional conflict situations as time allows. Devote follow-up sessions to this activity until the students demonstrate that they have internalized the problem-solving process and the concept of win-win solutions.

Discussion Questions

1. *Why is conflict usually unpleasant?*
2. *What makes people disagree about things?*
3. *What would life be like if we all agreed on everything?*
4. *Why are win-win solutions the best kind?*
5. *Can you think of a situation where a win-win solution would not be best?*

How to Create Win-Win Solutions to Conflict

Conflicts are normal. Everybody has them. Smart people don't try to settle conflicts by hitting, pushing, yelling, or calling each other names. They settle conflicts like they would any other problem. By creating a win-win solution—one that works for both (or all) of the people involved. Below are guidelines for creating win-win solutions. Follow these guidelines whenever you have a conflict.

Win-Win Process

1. Calm down.

2. Take turns describing the problem and your feelings.

3. Restate the other person's view to show that you understand.

4. Brainstorm possible solutions.

5. Talk about the solutions. Decide which ones are win-win.

6. Pick the best win-win solution (one in which both people get some or all of what they want).

7. Agree to implement the solution. Shake on it.

How to Make a New Friend

The best way to have a friend is to be a friend.
—UNKNOWN

Objectives

The students will:
1. Identify ways to make new friends.
2. Define the term clique and describe the effects of cliques.
3. Commit to including one new person in their group of friends.

Materials

One copy of the experience sheet, "Is It Worth It To Be In?," for each student

Procedure

Have the students form two teams. Give the teams 10 to 15 minutes to brainstorm lists describing ways to make new friends. At the end of the allotted time, reconvene the class and ask the groups to share their lists. Possible ideas include:

- Sit beside someone different in the cafeteria and say hello.
- Offer to show someone new around the school.
- Join a school organization.
- Offer to help someone with homework.
- Team up with someone you don't know very well to work on a class project.
- Run an ad in the school paper for someone to hike, bicycle or play tennis with.
- Ask someone you know to introduce you to new people.
- Go to the gym or track after school and say hello to the kids who are practicing.

Now write the word *clique* on the board and ask the students to define it. One possible definition might be:

An in-crowd or group of kids that defines itself as much by who is excluded as by who is included.

Discuss how a clique's policy of exclusion causes members to have difficulty making new friends by frustrating the efforts of someone who is not in the clique to become good friends with someone who is. Stress that the reason many kids want to be a part of a clique is to be liked by "important" people and feel important themselves.

Distribute the experience sheet, "Is It Worth It To Be In?" Allow the students about 10 minutes to complete the sheet. Then ask them to rejoin the teams and (voluntarily) share their answers to the questions.

Write the words "Smile—Ask—Listen" on the board. Suggest that this trio of words represents a great recipe for making friends. (Compare it to the safety adage, "Stop—Look—Listen.") A smile brightens the day for those who give and receive it. Asking questions gets conversations started and lets people know that you are interested in them. And through listening you learn things about the other person and show that you care.

Encourage the students to commit to making one new friend before the next session, or including one new person in their existing group of friends. Stipulate that before they can claim to have completed this assignment, the students must do something tangible with the new friend, such as sit together at an assembly, eat lunch together, go jogging or bicycling together, visit each other's home, see a movie together, or play video games after school. Ask the students to pay particular attention to the "clique phenomenon" and avoid doing anything that causes other people to feel left out.

Discussion Questions

1. *What qualities make a good friend?*
2. *Is it difficult or easy for people to become your friend? Why?*
3. *In what ways do you think cliques are good?*
4. *In what ways are cliques harmful?*
5. *Have you ever wanted to belong to a clique? If so, why was it important?*

Is It Worth It To Be In?

What have you done to be included in a group?

I have:

____Yes ____No ...Risked losing friends.

____Yes ____No ...Hurt people who thought they were my friends by making them feel left out.

____Yes ____No ...Done something I thought was not right.

____Yes ____No ...Done something I knew was against the law.

____Yes ____No ...Drunk alcohol or used drugs.

____Yes ____No ...Done something that might have harmed me physically.

____Yes ____No ...Done something that cost me a lot of money.

____Yes ____No ...Done something that interfered with my school work.

____Yes ____No ...Done something my parents would have objected to if they had known.

____Yes ____No ...Done whatever was necessary, as long as it didn't harm anyone else.

____Yes ____No ...Done something that was against my religion.

____Yes ____No ...Done whatever was necessary.

Can you remember a time when you were pressured to exclude someone from an activity?

How did you feel? _____

What did you do? _____

_____

_____

_____

If this ever happens again, what do you think you will do? _____

_____

_____

_____

_____

Speaking Out Against Bullying

The success of our living is measured not by what we can accumulate for ourselves, but what we can bestow upon our fellow travelers on life's tough trail.
—W. PHILLIP KELLER

Objectives

The students will:
1. Identify interventions they can make to stop bullying and hurtful behavior.
2. Recognize that maintaining a peaceful, respectful school climate is everyone's responsibility.

Materials

One copy of the experience sheet, "Stop Bullying! It's Everyone's Responsibility!," for each student

Procedure

Point out that incidents of bullying and hurtful behavior that happen at school often occur in busy places, like hallways, lunch areas, in front of the school and on playgrounds. Although adults don't usually see these things happen, very often other kids are nearby and do witness the incidents, but don't know what to do.

Ask the students to help you brainstorm things that witnesses can do to stop students from bullying one another. Add the following four ideas if they are not mentioned by the group.

1. Confront the person who is bullying. Say something like, "Leave Sally alone. It's wrong to talk mean to others."
2. If the hurtful person is just showing off, don't give him or her an audience. Walk away.
3. If appropriate and safe, distract the kids involved.
4. Create safety in numbers. If you know that a particular student is often harassed, put down, bullied or treated meanly, make sure that the victim is not alone in places where he or she is vulnerable.
5. Report fights and other violent acts.

Write the following headings on the board:

Who   How

Stress that students should talk to an adult about every incident of bullying or violence that occurs. Under the "Who" heading, list appropriate adults.

Discuss ways of reporting that guard the safety of students, such as writing an anonymous note, going to the office after school when the rest of the kids have gone home, or calling a teacher or counselor at home. List these ideas under "How." Make a distinction between tattling and snitching and reporting an incident. Tattling is about wanting to get someone in trouble. Informing an adult is about wanting to help the victim.

Distribute the experience sheets and go over the directions. Define any words with which the children might not be familiar. After allowing the students time to complete the sheet, ask volunteers to read their top five ideas. Facilitate discussion. Try to honor and implement ideas that seem workable, developing action plans, as needed.

Discussion Questions

1. *Why do people bully and say and do hurtful things to one another?*
2. *What would you do if you saw your best friend being hurtful to someone?*
3. *What would you do if you saw a student you didn't know bullying someone?*
4. *When you feel angry at someone, what can you do to avoid being mean or disrespectful?*
5. *How can we have a peaceful school where everyone respects everyone else?*

Stop Bullying!
It's Everyone's Responsibility

It is up to everyone in the school to stop hurtful, bullying behavior. When you and other students decide that it is time to stand up to kids who try to hurt others, you can really make a difference. When you mobilize and take action, you can help put an end to bullying. Wouldn't you like to have a caring, peaceful school?

What can be done to stop kids from harassing each other? List your ideas here:

_____
_____
_____
_____
_____

What can you do?

_____
_____
_____
_____
_____

Cross out any ideas that involve violence or retaliation. Don't ever do what you want the other person to stop doing. Besides, violence usually makes things worse.

Go back and look at each of your ideas. Ask yourself, "Will this idea really work?" Cross out any ideas that simply will not work.

Now, pick your five best ideas and number them #1 to #5. Make your very best idea #1. That's the idea you should try first when you see someone being mean to another kid!

No More Put Downs

*Time goes by so fast, people go in and out of your life.
You must never miss the opportunity to tell these people how much they mean to you.*
—FROM "CHEERS"

Objectives

The students will:
1. Become aware of a common communication habit that is often hurtful to others and can damage relationships.
2. Understand reasons that people put down others.
3. Empathize with the receiver of put-down statements.

Procedure

Tell the class that you want to focus on a way of talking that is very common at school. Explain that talking this way often starts out as a form of joking around, or teasing, and then turns into a habit. Unfortunately, this habit of communication can be hurtful to others and serves no real purpose. Ask the students to guess what you are talking about. Give them a few moments and if no one guesses correctly, write "put downs" or "putting others down" on the board.

Ask the students to help you make a list of all the statements they remember hearing people say that put others down. As the students give you the words, write them on the board, enclosing each phrase in quotation marks.

Talk about the nature of put-downs. Ask the students:

— *Why do people put each other down?*
— *Are some put downs worse than others?*
— *How can a person tell the difference between a put down that is meant as a joke and a put down that is intentionally hurtful?*

Give the students the following assignment: *For the next 24 hours, carry a pencil and a piece of paper with you and write down every put-down statement you hear. Write down put downs that are directed at you, and put downs that you overhear between others. Record put downs that you hear on TV shows too. Bring your list to our next session.*

At the next session have the students take out their put-down surveys. Go around the room and have each student act out two items from his or her list, mimicking as closely as possible the method of delivery they witnessed when they observed the put down. To assure a broad sampling, instruct them to avoid repeating the substance of any previously shared put down. (If you have prepared the students adequately they will have numerous examples, since put downs are extremely common.)

When everyone has had a turn to contribute, ask if there are any additional put downs that should be added to the list. Then go back and categorize and tally the examples. Here are three possible categories:

1. Reflex put downs (often an unconscious habit)
2. Teasing or joking put downs
3. Malicious (intentionally hurtful) put downs

Discuss the different motivations that lead to each type of put down, emphasizing that all types are often interpreted by the receiver as intentionally hurtful and can damage friendships.

Now ask the students to think of positive responses that could be substituted for habitual and joking put downs. Choose two or three put downs from those shared and brainstorm ways to change the wording or the object of the put down so that it is no longer hurtful.

Give the students a few minutes to write a positive substitute for at least two of the put downs on their 24-hour surveys. Go around the group and ask the students to share what they have written. Ask the students to act out the positive substitutes in the same way they did the put downs.

Discussion Questions

1. *Where do we learn put downs?*
2. *How do put-downs make people feel?*
3. *What would be the effect on this group if we were always putting each other down?*
4. *How should you respond to people who put you down?*
5. *How can you break the habit of putting others down?*
6. *How do positive, affirming statements make people feel?*
7. *What would be the effect on this group if we said mostly positive, affirming things to each other?*
8. *Why don't we say positive, affirming things more often?*

Gossip Hurts

Our deeds still travel with us from afar, and what we have been makes us what we are.
—GEORGE ELIOT

Objectives

The students will:
1. Identify categories and topics of conversation.
2. Estimate how much conversational time they devote to gossip.
3. Describe the effects of gossip on themselves and others.
4. Recognize that they have many conversational choices, and need not resort to hurtful gossip.

Procedure

On the board, write the headings, "Things," "People," "Activities," and "Ideas." Explain that most conversations center on one of these broad subject areas. Ask the students to think of their own conversations and brainstorm typical topics that fall under each heading, such as:

Things
- clothing
- houses and cars
- video games and computers
- toys and sports equipment

People
- relationships, who's going with whom, marriages, divorces, etc.
- celebrities and people in the news
- friends, family
- gossip about any of the above

Activities
- sports and games
- TV shows and movies
- parties, dances, other social events
- studying, reading, computing
- shopping

Ideas
- thoughts about life
- politics, spiritual beliefs, current events
- history, art, music, scientific discoveries

- insights about self and others
- solutions to problems, creative ways of doing things

Ask the students to individually estimate the percentage of their conversations that deal with each category. Ask a few volunteers to share their estimates with the group.

Next, zero in on the term *gossip*. Ask the students to define it. Write their ideas on the board. Add a dictionary definition if you think it will help. Here's an American Heritage definition: *rumor or talk of a personal, sensational or intimate nature.*

Spend the remainder of the session discussing the role and impact of gossip in the social world of the students. Use the questions below to stimulate thought and discussion. Encourage the students to express their feelings, experiences and opinions, but caution them not to repeat specific gossip or to use real names.

Conclude the discussion by referring back to the list of categories and topics, and pointing out how many stimulating things there are to talk about that don't hurt anyone.

Discussion Questions

1. *Why do people gossip? What do we get out of it?*
2. *What are the dangers of gossiping?*
3. *Have you ever been hurt by gossip? What happened?*
4. *Has someone you know been hurt by gossip? How?*
5. *Have you ever repeated some gossip and then found out it wasn't true? What, if anything, did you do about it?*
6. *Do you think you are a gossip?*
7. *Do your peers think of you as a gossip?*
8. *Do you knowingly exaggerate gossip when repeating it?*
9. *How does the gossip of males differ from that of females? Who gossips more?*
10. *Do you know someone who refuses to repeat gossip, and who doesn't seem interested in hearing it?*
11. *When does gossip become an addiction?*
12. *Have you ever refused to pass along a titillating bit of gossip? Why?*
13. *When someone tells you they have gossip to share, how do you usually react?*
14. *Have you ever refused to listen to a bit of gossip?*

Making the Right Decision

*We have to accept the consequences of every deed,
word and thought throughout our lifetime.*
—ELIZABETH KUBLER ROSS

Objectives

The students will:
1. Differentiate right choices from wrong choices.
2. Identify different methods of evaluating behavior.
3. Recognize inner conflict over doing the right thing.
4. Describe times when they did the right thing.

Materials

Several 3X5 cards for each student

Procedure

Begin by explaining to the students that this activity is about how decisions are made, and about deciding to do what's right in situations that call for moral judgment. In your own words state:

Every time you take an action of any kind, that action is preceded by a decision. So you are making decisions constantly. Sometimes the decisions seem automatic, like the decision to sit at your desk, or wave to a friend across the room. Other times, the decision requires some thought. Maybe you have different choices, like whether to study or play games on your computer. However, if your mom told you not to play games until your homework was finished, then it would be right to study, and wrong to play games. Many decisions involve choosing between right and wrong behaviors. Sometimes the difference between right and wrong is very clear. Other times it is more difficult to figure out.

Present the following dilemma to the students:

You are in a store with two friends, Chris and Lee, looking at some neat merchandise. Lee disappears down a nearby aisle. After a few minutes, you decide to join Lee. When you turn the corner, you see Lee slip a package into his backpack. You also see a store employee a few yards away who apparently saw the same thing you did. You stop in your tracks and quickly back up, wondering what to do.

Ask the students, *What are your choices?*

List their ideas on the board. Encourage them to see numerous possibilities, including:

- Go back and rejoin Chris, hoping the store employee didn't notice you.
- Go back, grab Chris and head for the door, hoping that Lee will be all right and will join you later.
- Grab Lee and run for the door.
- Walk over and quietly urge Lee to put the package back because someone is watching.
- Urge Lee to put the package back because stealing is wrong.
- Try to distract the employee with a question.
- Stand your ground and wait to see what happens. If the employee confronts Lee, tell the truth about what you saw.
- Wait to see what happens. If the employee intervenes, pretend you don't know Lee.

When the students run out of ideas, go back and discuss the options. Talk about what's right and wrong with each idea, and what might happen as a result of each choice.

Distribute the 3x5 cards. Read aloud one of the remaining situations. Give the students a few minutes to write down on a card a brief description of what they would do. Collect the cards and read each one aloud without divulging the writer's name. Make notes on the board about the various choices mentioned.

Again, engage the students in a discussion about what's right and wrong in the situation, and the possible consequences of various choices.

Follow the same procedure with the other story.

Story 1

> On the last day of school, Mark gets his parents' permission to walk home through a large park with his friend Henry, rather than take the school bus. Though Mark promises to stay on the marked hiking trails, Henry talks him into taking a short cut up a remote wooded area to get to their neighborhood. Part way through, the boys are attacked by a swarm of bees. The bees chase and sting them. Henry, who doesn't run as fast as Mark, gets the worst of it. At the first house they come to, they are given shelter and first aid, and the owner calls their parents, police and paramedics. While the paramedics are preparing to take Henry to the hospital, Henry whispers tearfully to Mark not to tell anyone they went off the trail. The police officer wants to know where

the attack took place so he can send an exterminator to kill the bees and determine if the hive belonged to dangerous Africanized or killer bees. Mark's parents want reassurance that their son obeyed their orders. Mark is torn. He doesn't think it's fair to kill the bees. If he says he and Henry were on the trail, the exterminator probably won't find the hive and he and Henry won't get into any trouble. But if they don't find the hive, they won't know if the bees are Africanized. He's also worried about Henry, whose father is very strict. If you were Mark, what would you do?

Story 2

Tami plays first clarinet in her school's award-winning band. The band has been raising money for over two years to take a concert tour of schools in Europe. The trip will start during Spring vacation, but continue a week longer, so only those musicians with a B average or better will be allowed to go. Tami is right on the edge. She must get an A on the upcoming Algebra test in order to get a B in math, and without a B in math she will lose out on the trip. Tami's friend Art, also a band member, works out a code that will enable him and two other classmates to signal Tami with the correct answers. He insists that the co-conspirators rehearse the system at his house the night before the test. Tami is a good student and has always done her own work. This scheme doesn't feel right, but she has her heart set on the trip. If you were Tami, what would you do?

Discussion Questions

1. *Why is it sometimes hard to make the right decision?*
2. *How often has fear of punishment, or fear of the consequences, caused you to make a wrong decision?*
3. *What determines whether a decision is right or wrong?*
4. *When should you ask for help in making a decision?*
5. *Does it take more courage to do the wrong thing and worry about getting caught, or to do the right thing and accept the consequences?*

What Is the Right Thing to Do?

If you want a quality, act as if you already had it.
WILLIAM JAMES

Objectives

The students will:
1. Identify moral values underlying the decisions of children and adults in ordinary situations.
2. Discuss alternative behaviors in each of the situations.
3. Recognize how values guide actions.

Materials

Copies of the dilemmas for distribution (optional, depending on method of implementation)

Procedure

These stories or dilemmas may be used in several ways. Here are four suggestions:

- Occasionally read a dilemma aloud to the students. Ask the discussion questions. Help the students to identify the values inherent in the situation, evaluate the motives and actions of the characters, and consider alternative courses of action.
- Divide the class into small groups and give each group a copy of one dilemma (including discussion questions). Have the groups read and discuss their dilemma, answering the questions. Ask each group in turn to summarize its dilemma and conclusions for the rest of the class.
- Divide the class into small groups and give each group a copy of one dilemma. Have each group develop, rehearse and deliver a role play of its dilemma for the rest of the class. After each role play, ask the discussion questions, allowing the entire class to respond. Brainstorm alternative actions in each situation and ask the performing group to role play one or two of those.
- Modify the following dilemmas or create your own to best meet the interests of your students.

Dilemma #1.

Well before the season is over, Peterson High School wins the division basketball title. Everyone is very excited and looking forward to the playoffs; however, there are still two games left to play in the regular season. When five players (all seniors and top players) fail to show up for those two final games, the coach refuses to let the team compete in the playoffs.

The fans are bitterly disappointed. The parents (particularly parents of the players) are furious and protest the coach's decision to the school board. During the hearing, it comes out that the five players skipped the game intentionally, and that the rest of the team knew of their plans in advance. Having already won the title, these "stars" didn't feel like playing weak teams, and thought that the rest of the team could handle it. If they lost, so what? The two games weren't that important.

After several hours of testimony, the school board caves in to the demands of the parents and orders the coach to resume practices for the playoffs. The coach refuses and resigns.

Discussion Questions:

1. What are the moral values in this situation?
2. How would you feel if you were a student at Peterson High School?
3. What lesson was the coach trying to teach when he refused to let the team play?
4. How would you have voted if you were a member of the school board?
5. Why did the coach resign?

Dilemma #2.

Yvonne, a computer engineer, tells Alex, her coworker, that she is going to quit her job within a few weeks, but swears Alex to secrecy. This troubles Alex because he thinks Yvonne should let their manager know as soon as possible. Yvonne has many responsibilities and Alex feels it's unfair to spring it on the department at the last minute. Nevertheless, Sam agrees to keep Yvonne's secret. When Yvonne finally quits, the boss is upset and asks Alex, "Did you know about this?" Alex believes that if he tells the truth his boss will be very angry. He answers, "No, this is the first I've heard of it."

Discussion Questions:

1. What are the moral values in this situation?
2. If you were Alex, what would you have done when Yvonne told you her plan?
3. What was more important in this situation, not betraying Yvonne's trust, or telling the manager so that the company could prepare for Yvonne's leaving?
4. What do you think would have happened if Alex had told his manager the truth instead of lying?
5. What's wrong with lying to protect yourself (like Alex did) if telling the truth won't change the situation anyway?

Dilemma #3.

Mr. Roberts hires a demolition company to take down his old house, so that he can build a new one. The demolition company sends in a crew of its best workers, but the manager gets busy and neglects to check on the workers during the first two days of the job. The workers find asbestos (a toxic substance) in the floor and walls. Instead of stopping the job and reporting the asbestos, they don't tell anyone and it gets mixed in with all the other materials. On the third day the manager discovers the mistake. He fires the crew chief and calls in a friend whose company specializes in removing asbestos safely. To save time (so that the demolition company doesn't lose money), the manager and his friend agree to tell Mr. Roberts that all the asbestos has been safely removed. In fact, they only remove a small amount of it. They throw the rest in the landfill, which is illegal. The demolition company finishes the job on time, all the workers get paid, and Mr. Roberts never finds out what really happened to the asbestos.

Discussion Questions:

1. *What are the moral values in this situation?*
2. *Whose fault was it that the asbestos was handled improperly?*
3. *Whose responsibility was it to make sure that the problem was corrected?*
4. *Was the manager right to fire the crew chief?*
5. *Which was more important: to finish the job profitably and on time, or to take extra days or weeks to find all of the asbestos and get rid of it safely?*

Dilemma #4.

Mee lives near Hendrix High School. Her jogging route takes her past the student parking lot, which is separated from the street by a tall chain-link fence. The inside of the chain-link fence is usually lined with trash several inches deep that blows across the lot and piles up along the bottom of the fence—candy wrappers, soft drink cups, lunch bags and discarded schoolwork. It's a disgusting sight.

One Monday morning while jogging, Mee notices two men in work clothes picking up the trash and putting it in the back of a truck. She jogs over and asks the men if they are school district employees. They answer yes. She asks, "Is it part of your job to pick up the trash that the students drop?" One of the men laughs sarcastically and answers, "Yes, Ma'am, we do this every Monday morning, and we clean up the trash at several other schools too."

A month later, the district asks voters to approve a bond measure worth millions of dollars to repair badly rundown classrooms. Mee organizes a "No on Prop A" committee and campaigns against the measure. She makes TV appearances, writes letters and talks to civic groups. She tells the story of the men who pick up the students' trash at taxpayer expense. She argues that the kids don't deserve better classrooms until they stop trashing the ones they have. The bond measure is defeated.

Discussion Questions:

1. What are the moral values in this story?
2. Whose responsibility is it to dispose of the students' trash?
3. Did Mee do the right thing by opposing the bond measure? Why or why not? What else could she have done?
4. Did the school district have an obligation to the neighborhood to do something about the trash? What could they have done?
5. If you were a student leader at Hendrix High School, what would you have done?

Dilemma #5.

Rose and Javier have been dating for several months. Brandon is best friends with Javier and a cousin to Rose. He suspects that Javier has started seeing another girl behind Rose's back. He says to Javier, "I thought Rose was your girl, but I keep seeing you with Linda. What gives?"

Javier says that he and Linda are just friends. But a few days later, Brandon sees Javier with his arm around Linda. Brandon confronts Javier again and tells him that if Javier doesn't level with Rose, he will tell her himself. Javier gets angry and tells Brandon to mind his own business. Brandon says that his cousin *is* his business and he can't stand by and let her get hurt. He gives Javier one week to straighten things out. After that he is going to tell Rose everything he knows.

Discussion Questions:

1. *What are the moral values in this situation?*
2. *If Brandon wants to remain friends with Javier and protect his cousin Rose at the same time, what are his options?*
3. *How much would you want to know if you were Rose?*
4. *How would you feel if you were Javier? What would you do?*
5. *When is it kind to be truthful with someone, even if the truth hurts?*

Dilemma #6.

Every year Laura organizes a big Thanksgiving celebration for her husband's large family and many employees. She prepares the menu, does the shopping, roasts three or four turkeys, rents extra tables, and tents the garden for the outdoor feast. She also complains a lot about the amount of work she has to do. The closer the holiday gets, the worse her mood becomes.

Laura's husband, Paul, is a very busy man and can't help her much. The holiday celebration is important to him, but his wife is more important. So this year as the holiday approaches, Paul suggests to Laura that they forget the big dinner and go to a nice restaurant instead, just the two of them. Laura says, "Why? Don't you want to entertain your family and staff?" Paul answers, "Of course I do, but it's so much work. I'm just thinking of you." Laura promises to think about it.

A few days later, Paul notices that his wife has begun making grocery lists for the big dinner. He asks, "Are you sure you want to do this?" Laura surprises him by answering, "Yes, I'm sure. This year instead of being grouchy, I've decided to be grateful. I'm grateful for you and our wonderful family, and I'm grateful that you have a successful business with lots of good employees. I figure if I concentrate on my gratitude, the work won't seem so difficult. I feel excited already."

Discussion Questions:

1. What are the moral values in this situation?
2. What made Laura change her attitude?
3. How did Paul's suggestion affect Laura's thinking?
4. Is gratitude a choice, or is it a feeling that just happens?
5. What have you chosen to be grateful for?

Dilemma #7.

An American gymnast wins the gold medal for best overall performance in the Olympic games. It's a stunning victory and the whole team celebrates. A short while later, officials discover that two judges failed to make required point deductions for mistakes that the American made. If those deductions had been made, the winner would have been the Korean competitor. However, because the official announcement has been made, it cannot be changed. The Olympic Committee fires the two judges, but the medal belongs to the American.

Many people urge the American to voluntarily give up the medal. They think it would be the honorable thing for him to do. But the rules say he has a right to keep the medal, and everyone agrees that he is an outstanding gymnast. After all, there was only a fraction of one point between his score and the Korean's. He decides to accept the medal and keep it. At the awards ceremony, many spectators boo the Americans.

Discussion Questions:

1. What are the moral values in this situation?
2. Was it right for the Olympic committee to fire the judges? Was it right of the crowd to boo the Americans? Why?
3. What would the American lose by voluntarily giving up the medal? What would he gain?
4. How would you feel if you were the Korean competitor? How would you feel if you were the American?
5. What is the fairest thing to do, abide by the official decision and keep the medal, or disregard the official decision and give it back?

Dilemma #8.

College roommates Omar, Will and Rich decide to take the weekend off and go camping. They pile in Will's car and head for the mountains, promising each other that they'll return early Sunday to study for a big math exam first thing Monday morning. In the mountains they meet another group of young people. The weekend is great fun. It's late Sunday night before they head back to the campus. All three are exhausted.

Omar and Will are worried about the exam, but Rich has a plan. He says, "First thing in the morning, I'll use my cell phone to call Professor Ford and tell her that Will's car broke down and we had to have it towed. I'll arrange for us to take a makeup exam. That way we'll have time to study.

When they go in for the makeup exam, Professor Ford announces that the exam is short—only three questions. Then she places each student in a separate room and hands them the exam. The questions are, 1) What was the name of the tow truck company? 2) What caused the car to break down? 3) At what time did you finally arrive home?

Discussion Questions:

1. *What are the moral values in this situation?*
2. *What was wrong with the plan Rich outlined?*
3. *What else could the guys have done?*
4. *Were Professor Ford's actions fair? Why or why not?*
5. *Why do we sometimes lie to avoid the consequences of our actions?*

Dilemma #9.

The small parking lot of Trader's, a popular market, is usually packed with cars. A large cart-return rack is located about halfway down each row of parking spaces. People who park near the front of the lot are better off returning their carts to the front of the store, which has two collection racks.

After Virginia unloads her groceries, she doesn't bother to look for a cart return area. Instead she pushes her cart into the neighboring parking space, which is empty at the moment. Later, Ralph can't pull his car all the way into the space without first getting out and moving the cart. In the meantime, his car blocks traffic in the aisle and other drivers start honking.

Melissa puts her baby and six-year-old in their car seats first, then unloads her groceries and pushes the cart between two parked cars, hitting both. (The cart return station is about 30 feet away.) When she gets into the car, her six-year-old says, "You're supposed to take the cart to the cart place, Mommy." She says, "To do that I'd have to leave you and your sister alone in the car."

Angie loads her groceries in the car first, before lifting her two-year-old out of the shopping cart. The empty cart starts rolling across the lot, quickly picking up speed. Supporting the baby on her hip, Angie runs after it. She finally catches the cart on the far side of the lot and pushes it back to the return station. Both Angie and the baby are laughing.

Discussion Questions:

1. *What are the moral values in this situation?*
2. *Why did Virginia leave her shopping cart in the middle of the lot? What were the consequences?*
3. *Why did Melissa refuse to return her cart? Do you agree with her reasoning? Why or why not?*
4. *Why did Angie run after her cart? Did she do the right thing? Why or why not?*
5. *Who is affected when people abandon their shopping carts? What can happen?*

Dilemma #10.

Lucia invites two close girlfriends over to celebrate her 11th birthday. They arrive in the afternoon to swim in the pool, and plan to stay overnight. All the splashing and laughter attracts the attention of Emma, who lives next door. Emma is a year younger than Lucia and goes to a private school, so she doesn't know the other girls. When Emma comes to the front door, Lucia's mom invites her in and sends her out to the pool area. Emma says hi and tries to be friendly, but Lucia is upset. She wants to celebrate with her school friends. She sees Emma as an intruder and doesn't want her around.

Lucia whispers to her friends to ignore Emma so she'll go away. Her mother, who is watching from inside the house, sees the girls turn their backs on Emma. After a few minutes, Lucia's mother calls her inside. She says, "You are being rude to Emma. She and her parents are good neighbors and we should treat them kindly."

Lucia says, "But Mom, this is my birthday party and I didn't invite Emma. I should be able to decide which kids to include."

Lucia's mother thinks a minute and answers, "True, this isn't how we planned it, but this is how it turned out and you'll have to make the best of it. It's the caring thing to do." When Lucia starts to whine, her mom adds firmly, "Either you include Emma in the fun or I'm sending everyone home. It's your choice."

Discussion Questions:

1. *What are the moral values in this situation?*
2. *What do you think of Lucia's actions? What else could she have done?*
3. *Should Lucia be allowed to have things exactly the way she wants them on her birthday? Why or why not?*
4. *What was Emma's responsibility in this situation?*
5. *Was Lucia's mom right to intervene and tell Lucia what to do? Was she right to threaten her? What could she have done differently to get a better reaction from Lucia?*

If your heart is in Social-Emotional Learning, visit us online.

Come see us at
www.InnerchoicePublishing.com

Our web site gives you a look at all our other Social-Emotional Learning-based books, free activities, articles, research, and learning and teaching strategies. Every week you'll get a new Sharing Circle topic and lesson.

15079 Oak Chase Court
Wellington, FL 33414

www.ingramcontent.com/pod-product-compliance
Lightning Source LLC
Chambersburg PA
CBHW081925170426
43200CB00014B/2833